HOW TO DESTROY
A TECH STARTUP

in Three Easy Steps

Cover design © Leah McCloskey

Book design by Emi Lotto

ISBN 978-0-9989976-1-2

10 9 8 7 6 5 4 3 2 1

HOW TO DESTROY
A TECH STARTUP

in Three Easy Steps

Lawrence Krubner
& Natalie Sidner

NOTE

For the sake of brevity, a large number of incidents were cut from the book. Anyone interested in more detail can look here:

http://www.smashcompany.com/business/how-to-destroy-a-tech-startup-in-three-easy-steps

INTRODUCTION

Ninety percent of all new businesses die. Even when based on brilliant ideas, the hard work and creativity of the team often comes to naught. Why?

Emotions can hinder or uplift. We might hope that those in leadership positions possess strength and resilience, but vanity and fragile egos have sabotaged many of the businesses that I've worked with. Defeat is always a possibility, and not everyone finds healthy ways to deal with the stress.

Each person matters. Established firms will have a bureaucracy that can ensure some stability, even when an eccentric individual is in a leadership position, but when a company consists of just two or three people, and one of them reacts neurotically to challenges, the company is doomed.

From 2002 to 2008 I worked with an entrepreneur who had inherited a few million dollars when he was twenty-five. He admired musicians and considered the music industry glamorous, so he built a sound studio. It never made money. The bands that stopped by were broke. Those few who came up with a hit song mostly signed with a major label which, typically, had its own recording studio.

I met him in 2002 when his focus was shifting to the Web. I had developed some software that allowed people to create weblogs. Typepad, which fostered something similar to what I'd built, had just raised $23 million in funding. Surely we could do the same?

Our difficulties were self-imposed. We might go like maniacs on some project for four months, and when we were on the brink of unveiling it to the public, he would grow bored with it and move on to something else. The first time this happened, and I asked him his reasons, he improvised some arguments that sounded plausible; there were already too many startups doing the same thing. But this pattern, where he walked away from a project just when we were ready to introduce it to the public, repeated itself.

What led to this self-sabotage? As I met his whole family over the years I got to see the sad dynamics that ate at him. A modest business success would not be enough, in fact, it would leave him embarrassed. Only the creation of something as big as Google would suffice. But to grow that big, we would first need to be small, and that was the step he had no patience for.

As the years went by and he burned away all the money he'd inherited, the stress wrecked him. His self-image became increasingly grandiose. He told people that he was a visionary, someone who was able to tell what the future would look like. Late at night he would smoke weed and read articles on Slashdot and TechCrunch and then put together an amalgam of words that seemed full of the bright hopes of humanity, which he offered up as our marketing: "The Universe is fundamentally electromagnetic yet non-sentient, and we are sentient but only partly electromagnetic; the Internet is the ultimate harnessing of sentience to the fundamental forces of the Universe. Therefore our software will put you, our customer, in the driver's seat of real-time conscious human evolution." Later, when he wrote up our business plan, he put these two sentences in the executive summary. I'm not joking.

He had no capacity for internal dialogue. Only by talking to others could he hear his own thoughts. At our peak in 2007, we had eight people on our team. Sometimes I would look around the room when he was talking at everyone, and I would think, "If you add up what we pay all these people, we are spending $300 an hour so that he can have an audience." When he was fearful about our chances of success, he would need to talk to everyone, and when he was euphoric about our chances of success, he would need to talk to everyone. Therapy would have been cheaper.

We had one modest success, in 2007. His girlfriend, a yoga instructor, suggested we build an online marketplace where yoga instructors could sell videos, as well as offer health advice. This site was an immediate success. Within the first month it was profitable. We were written up in all of the major yoga magazines. It seemed obvious to me that we should use the same technology to build a series of similar sites. We could do a site devoted to cooking videos, another devoted to tennis, another devoted to golf. Indeed, just a few years later, the team behind Revolutiongolf.com did exactly what we could have done.

My business partner, however, was enraged by the success of the yoga site. He had burned through several million dollars chasing ideas that he felt were "visionary" and then his girlfriend came up with a simple idea that turned into our one true hit. To this day, it remains a popular yoga site. We could have built an empire around that site, but instead his girlfriend's success left him bitter.

I finally ended the partnership in 2008 after I had decided that I could never build anything successful while I worked with him. A decade later, he has not yet built the giant success that he fantasizes about, but he is still active in the local tech scene. If you run a Google search for "Charlottesville Ted Talk Archaeomediaology," you can see that he is still trying to sell his vision.

I wish I could say that this situation was all together unique, but I've found that self-sabotage is remarkably common. When inexperienced entrepreneurs ask my advice about their idea for a tech startup, they often worry "What if Google decides to compete with us? They will crush us!" I respond that far more startups die of suicide than homicide. And I'm hardly the only one who has noticed this odd fact. The great business guru Peter Drucker made the point repeatedly. In his 1985 book Innovation and Entrepreneurship, Drucker includes a long chapter on the tendency of entrepreneurs to destroy the innovation they'd created.

I could tell that story, but recently I was an eye-witness to an even more extreme case. By 2015 I had moved to New York City. The chance to work on a uniquely innovative project filled me with excitement, and in fact I was so thrilled by the work that I was slow to recognize how deeply dysfunctional the leadership was. The story of this doomed Big Apple startup, written in day-by-day format, occupies the rest of this book. From the trenches, at close range, what does it look like when a brilliant idea begins to die? What are the warning signs that stress is beginning to undermine people's rationality, that decisions are being warped by ego and insecurity? Humans can be messy, and other people's messiness is often entertaining. Sometimes it is even educational.

MONDAY, MAY 4TH, 2015

My most recent startup—a question-and-answer site along the lines of Stack Exchange or Yahoo Answers—had just failed, and I was broke. One of the great advantages of being unemployed is that you can finally catch up on all the pop-culture references that your friends make. I'd never seen the show *Mad Men* but my friends and co-workers often talked about it, so I spent a week watching all seven seasons. Then I watched the three seasons available of Lena Dunham's show *Girls*.

As fun as it was to watch all the shows that I'd heard about but never seen, there came a point when I began to think I should find some sort of job. I sent word to my friends, people I'd worked with before. A few dozen suggestions came back about various startups. Unfortunately, most of them seemed frivolous: a dating app, an event planning app, a restaurant reservation system. The world was already suffering a glut of dating apps and restaurant apps. I wanted to join a project that I could believe in.

I reached out to a talent agency, and they asked me to go talk to a guy named John. I met him at the ThinkCoffee just south of Union Square.

At twenty-two years of age, John was a dynamo of energy, bursting with excitement about his new startup, Celolot. He'd formed it the year before with two friends of his, Dennis (the main computer programmer) and Griffin (the iPhone expert).

"We think we have a really unique idea here," he said with a note of promise. Thin and brown-haired, dressed in business casual, he moved around a lot in his chair. His eyes were bright and he seemed super excited about his new endeavor.

"That's fantastic," I responded politely. "But when it comes to startups, execution matters as much as originality."

"Absolutely!" He nodded. "We agree one hundred percent. That's why we want to put together a really good team."

"That's the key, especially at the start. I had my own startup for six years. You know what I learned? A single weak player can cripple the whole team."

"Exactly! Everyone needs to be strong! We want to have a team full of

2

rockstars!"

So it seemed we were starting out in agreement on the issue of talent.

"Tell me about your company," I said.

He laid it on me. Most salespeople are human-centered and enjoy talking with other individuals—but they hate dealing with computers. If a salesperson is selling shampoo to Sheraton Hotels, the best part of their day will be talking to the customer; the worst part will be when they have to go back to the office and deal with their company's reporting software. More likely than not, this will be Salesforce, the most widely-used software for tracking sales.

Salesforce is ugly. The interface is clunky. The poor salesperson has to sit down, bring up the website, click on a bunch of buttons, and navigate through a bunch of forms. The worst day of high school math was probably more fun for them.

Celolot aimed to change that. Instead of dealing with Salesforce, the salesperson would simply pull out their phone and send a text message to the Celolot system. For example, "Spoke to Carol. I just sold 1 million bottles of shampoo to Sheraton Hotels, rev 500000. Contract August 1. Delivery September 1." We would use a set of computer techniques known as Natural Language Processing, or NLP, to take a message like that and pull out all the fields that were significant to Salesforce:

Contact: Carol Harrington
Customer: Sheraton Hotels
Product: Shampoo
Quantity: 1,000,000
Revenue: $500,000
Close Date: August 1
Delivery Date: September 1

Celolot would automatically identify who sent the message, connect it with their Salesforce account, and log the information in the system. Salespeople would never have to interact with Salesforce directly.

Apart from streamlining the reporting process for Salesforce specifically, Celolot could potentially become the default interface for all sales-reporting software (a category officially known as Customer Relationship Managers, or CRMs, of which Salesforce and Pipedrive are two well-known examples). That would be game changing.

On a personal level, Celolot was exciting because it gave me the chance to work on the cutting edge of the technology industry. At various times, to make some quick cash, I had done plenty of boring corporate work. This would be different. This was a project I could believe in, something that might someday have a big impact on how business was conducted in the USA, and eventually around the world.

I also liked that Celolot was focused on businesses as potential customers. There had been too many consumer-oriented startups in recent years, most of which made their money by selling advertisements. As Jeff Hammerbacher, once the lead data scientist at Facebook, famously complained, "The best minds of my generation are thinking about how to make people click ads."[1] Celolot was focused on creating plain English interfaces for the big databases on which corporations rely—an idea that could unlock a multibillion-dollar industry.

TUESDAY, MAY 5TH, 2015

John liked me, so he asked me to talk to his co-founder, Dennis, who was the CTO. What followed was a tad bizarre.

We spoke via video. Dennis was twenty-one and in his last week of college. "Congratulations!" I remarked. "You're almost to the finish line!"

"Thanks, man!" He laughed. "I can't believe it's almost over. Time really flies."

Dennis was future-oriented, ready to move on to the next chapter of his life. Which, as I was about to learn, did not include the startup he'd been building. Rather, he would be going to Google. I was puzzled about this but didn't harp on the issue.

After the initial chit-chat, he cleared his throat and commenced the interview portion of our video conference. "Uh, okay." He seemed confused about what to say. "John wanted me to ask you some questions."

"Fire away," I said.

"Okay, look, uh …" He started, then paused. "How about this: You're in line at a barbershop. There are x number of barbers who all cut hair at different speeds, and there are y number of people ahead of you in line. Can you write the code to figure out how long you have to wait before you get a haircut?"

"You want me to write some code or just talk it through?"

"You can just talk it through."

An easy puzzle, which I worked out to his satisfaction. He asked me another: "Suppose you had to write the control system for an elevator. How many different commands would you need?"

Again, I gave him an answer that he found acceptable. He hit me with a few more.

Students get hit with these questions all the time. Dennis had probably just spent the last four years of his life answering one puzzle question after another. Perhaps he thought this was what professional computer programming consisted of. Me, I never think about puzzles ... except when I'm in job interviews. I would have found it more interesting to talk about some of the better projects that I've worked on, but he was calling the shots so I went along with it. And then suddenly he brought the interview an end: "Okay, I got to go."

"Uh, okay. You don't want to ask me anything about what I've done in the past?"

"No worries, man," he said, "You're good."

The nonchalance baffled me. I was his first hire. Where was his concern?

Later that day I went to a job interview at Time Warner, in the big office buildings at Columbus Circle. The people were very nice, and the pay was reasonable, but the work seemed dull: upload videos, organize videos, add categories to videos, follow the script written by the other programmers. I spoke to six different people over the course of three hours: a project manager, four computer programmers, and a designer I'd need to work with. At the end, they seemed eager to make me an offer, but said I had to talk to head of the department, who was not in that day. Could I come back next week? Sure, I said politely, but I had no intention of coming back. The place was too routine for me. A few days later they called me, hoping I would come back, so I said something generic about how I had chosen a different option.

The crew at Celolot seemed inexperienced, but I loved how ambitious their plan was.

WEDNESDAY, MAY 6TH, 2015

It was 11:00 A.M. and I was into my second cup of coffee when John called to tell me that they were offering me the job. He asked me to come in and sign paperwork the next day. My first day of work would be the twentieth.

Thursday, May 7th, 2015

Celolot was working out of the New York University startup incubator at 137 Varick Street, which housed numerous other early-stage start-ups. An incubator is both a physical space and a program; it supports entrepreneurs by providing management training, general mentoring, legal advice, and other services. In most ways, Silicon Valley is way ahead of any other startup ecosystem—but it was easy to forget that fact when I got to this incubator. Here were twenty-five small startups packed into a big room. There was a startup called RavenCart, trying to reinvent e-commerce. G-Code was a startup focused on teaching girls how to code. There were several startups, like Celolot, that wanted to use NLP to make big waves in various aspects of software. For instance, one startup was creating a plain-English search tool for travel ("I want the cheapest flight to Berlin, from New York, in October"). Voice of Law was another NLP startup aiming to build a next-generation search tool for finding legal precedents—a challenging task, since it would have to understand both plain English and the specialized jargon of the legal industry.

Back in 2011, Business Insider had a write-up about the incubator. In "Is The Varick Street NYU Poly Incubator The Best In NYC?", Jay Bhatti wrote:

> *After spending time at various incubators in the city, it very well may be that the Varick Street incubator is the top place in NYC for new entrepreneurs to call home. If you get the opportunity to be at Varick Street, you enjoy a lot of benefits. The incubator does not ask for any equity in your company. The rent is really affordable and includes a lot of amenities that are not free at other incubators. Best of all, you get access to high quality interns [and] employees from NYU, potential seed investors, NYU faculty advisors, and assistance from dozens of other private partners involved with the incubator. Probably one of the best benefits is that several serial entrepreneurs call the incubator home and serve as mentors and motivation for first time founders. For example, Stephanie Sarka (founding member of Overture), Jeff Giesea (founded and sold FierceMarkets), and David Sudolsky (experienced entrepreneur in the biotechnology space) are just some of the heavy hitters at Varick Street.*[2]

I eventually felt that Bhatti did not go far enough in listing all of the great features of this incubator.

John and I got coffee and sat down to talk. He told me that I'd be working with two other people at Celolot, whom they had just hired: Sital would be our NLP expert, and Hwan was an iPhone programmer who lived in Washington, DC and would be working with us primarily through teleconferences.

I was confused. Where were Dennis and Griffin?

John explained that Griffin was going out west to start an internship at Microsoft, and Dennis was headed out west to start an internship at Google.

So wait, they were doing internships even though they had a startup that had just been funded? How did that make sense?

John explained that the internships were set up long before any of them knew they were going to get funding.

Okay, but couldn't they cancel the internships? I mean, they had funding now. $1.3 million. Weren't they excited to dive in? Weren't they completely stoked to build their own startup?

Sure, totally, absolutely! John was eager to reassure me on that front. Dennis and Griffin were only going for ninety days and then they would be back. And they had promised to check in every week. They would be very present, even though they were out in California.

And the investors? I was puzzled. They were okay with this?

Sure, totally, absolutely! John didn't want me to worry about it. The investors were 100% supportive.

I walked home slowly and thought about what I had been told. Three guys in school come up with a clever idea. They go to a Salesforce convention. Even though these three guys have no track record and no product, someone gives them $1.3 million. As soon as they have the money, two of them leave. Was that believable?

Even weirder, these three guys all went to different schools. So how did they meet? Apparently John had found them. When? Why would he reach out to two strangers at different schools before he had come up with the idea for the startup? Surely I wasn't being told the whole story?

A small startup is either a transparent learning organization or it is dead. When you have a team of four or five people, with each person struggling to learn as much as possible every day, radical honesty is the only way to ensure that everyone is sharing the information that might be crucial to success. A startup faces innumerable obstacles, and a dishonest startup faces still more.

Tuesday, May 12th, 2015

John was hoping that Dennis and Griffin would visit New York City at least once, so I could meet them in person. They never did. Each of them was preparing for their move out west: packing their apartments, saying goodbye to their college friends, driving their stuff across the country.

Dennis finally sent me his documentation, along with access to the GitHub repository where he had all the code stored. GitHub is a popular service that allows programmers to keep track of each change they make to their software, making it easy to roll back to earlier versions in case of a mistake. It's like having an undo button that can go back in time as far as needed, even to versions of your software from months earlier.

The code was only a rough prototype, no more than three or four days worth of work. When they said they'd been working on the project for a year, I had to assume they'd been brainstorming for a year. Clearly, in terms of actual work, they'd done very little.

Thursday, May 21st, 2015

John sent this email to all of us:

Perks: HEY GUYS! Being the progressive startup we are, I want to hear from you guys how we can continue moving in that direction. Some of these perks can start very soon, and some not until we hire a bit more, start making sales, etc. However, I want to know what's important to you all.

The email contained a poll, and we were to vote on which perks we wanted. The possibilities included:

e-Books
Using an e-book or audiobook service, employees can learn new skills

and pursue higher education.

	1	2	3	4	5	
Not for me						HECK YES!

Cleaning Service
No one wants to work all day just to come home and have to clean their house.

	1	2	3	4	5	
Not for me						HECK YES!

Healthcare

	1	2	3	4	5	
Not for me						HECK YES!

Coffee & Tea
A daily cup of coffee or tea is a necessity for almost any employee.

	1	2	3	4	5	
Not for me						HECK YES!

There were many others. I voted for the cleaning service. This email gave me the impression that Celolot was very well funded. In fact, it's possible that the email was sent to us for precisely that reason: so we would have the impression of affluence.

These perks were never mentioned again.

In the afternoon, John and Sital and I sat in a little cluster and had an informal discussion about the nuances of Natural Language Processing (NLP). John was almost twitching with excitement. He talked rapidly and his hands moved around almost as fast as he spoke. Unlike Dennis, John struck me as properly enthusiastic about launching his own startup.

I was stunned by how little Sital knew. I'd assumed we'd hired a real expert, but he was struggling to understand basic concepts of computer programming. After an hour of talk, I realized his background was mostly in math. While math would be important to what we would be doing, we needed someone who could write code. The notion that he could learn all he needed in a short amount of time struck me as a considerable gamble.

Google employs some of the greatest NLP experts on the planet, and they have made extensive efforts to ensure that their search engine can understand your question, no matter how you phrase it. Imagine someone goes to Google and types:

How to de-rust cast iron pan

Even if it's not grammatically correct, the implications of a hyphenated word where the prefix denotes a negation have to be considered. These are the kinds of things that NLP takes into account. It's sort of like the theater stagehands who work hard behind the scenes to make sure the show goes smoothly when the curtain goes up. We all, as a society, take lightning-fast search results for granted and have no concept of the decades of work that have gone into birthing the phenomenon of NLP.

At Celolot, we were lucky in that we were dealing with such a specific niche. Salesforce was about business. There were only about a hundred verbs that we would have to worry about: sell, buy, agreed, close, meet, deliver, etc. Given the limited vocabulary, we would not need the resources of Google to pull this off.

FRIDAY, MAY 22ND, 2015

I wasn't yet sure of what the others would need, but it was clear we would need an API in the mix. Formally, "API" stands for Application Programming Interface, but computer programmers use those three letters as a kind of slang for any situation where software has to react to something. In our case, we needed software on our server that could react to the messages people sent from their iPhones. The API would coordinate the communications between all of the other software we would eventually build.

Monday, May 25th, 2015

I got to the incubator around 9:30 A.M. As this was the start of my first full week, I was still constantly looking around the space, absorbing everything I could. I was genuinely interested in what each startup at the incubator was working on. I eventually got to be friends with the folks at FieldOfFocus, who were building an amazing next-generation search tool for the stock photo industry. They had a team of three. Varak was the CTO, and he was like a Viking berserker warrior of code writing. There was an alcove at the back of the incubator with a couch in it; Varak would often code until 4:00 A.M., go sleep on the couch for three hours, then wake up and continue coding. He was building the whole frontend, the part of a website a user interacts with, and the whole backend, the technology that makes it all work. Lee, the FieldOfFocus CEO, gave me a demo of their search tool. Since my dad had been a professional photographer, I asked Lee to look for my dad's photos, and in five minutes he had found ten places where my dad's photos were being used on the Web.

My own experience trying to build a business was mostly a story of isolation and grinding loneliness. One reason that startup founders suffer so much depression and burnout is because they lose touch with their friends. This incubator seemed like a vastly superior way to grow a business, as there was a social element to simply being in the room.

Wednesday, May 27th, 2015

I was impressed with John's work ethic. Sometimes he was at the office as early as 7:00 A.M. I would usually arrive at 10:00 A.M., Starbucks in hand, and he would already be making what I assumed were cold calls. And for a product that did not even exist yet! He certainly was eager.

When I arrived that morning, John was on a video call. The man in the video was close to sixty years of age and very overweight. John was wearing headphones, so I could only hear half the conversation. John kept nodding his head and saying, "Okay, sure, I'll do it," and then a few moments later, "Okay, sure, totally. I will totally get to that." He sounded upbeat, which made me think the guy on screen was a potential customer.

After the call, I was told that the guy was named Milburn and was actually a member of the Celolot Board of Directors. Apparently, he'd had some suggestions for John about how to make the company better. I liked the idea that John had some active board members who were willing to give him advice.

I decided to abandon Dennis's code. This was an easy decision, since he had clearly built it as a throwaway. I was fairly confident that he, too, would have abandoned it if he had been working with us full time. Still, he was the CTO and it occurred to me that I should check with him. I sent him an email to explain what I was doing and I CC'd John on it.

A few minutes later, John spun around on me, alarmed.

"What are you doing?" he asked.

"Right now?" I wasn't sure what he meant. "An API app?"

"Why would you write to Dennis?"

"Because he is the CTO?"

"Oh!" John looked shocked. "Oh, okay. Right. But listen, he is doing a thing out west right now, so don't bother him."

"Cool. So, next time, I'll just make the decision myself?"

"Great. Yeah. Great."

I wondered how things would go when Dennis came back, after ninety days, and had to review all of the decisions that I had made. What if he disagreed with some of them? Or all of them? I supposed there was the assumption that he would defer to whatever decisions I had made. This seemed reasonable to me, both because he had abdicated his responsibilities, but also because I had the most real-world experience of anyone on the team, so it would be rational for them to accept my professional judgement.

Thursday, May 28th, 2015

College seems boring for some people, I suppose, whereas jumping into the real world is enticing (especially if someone offers you $1.3 million). John had planned to quit school to work on his company, but his parents were applying all the pressure they could to keep him moving toward his degree, and today was the first day of the summer semester. So Sital and I were at the incubator, but our CEO was not. Aside from our conversation about NLP, I knew nothing about Sital. This seemed like the right time to get to know him better. My plan was to invite him out to lunch but at lunchtime he was engrossed in a YouTube video about weightlifting. I figured I'd wait until he was done watching, but he just kept going, one video after another. We sat right next to each other for hours without any kind of interaction.

Observing Sital for the first time was interesting, to say the least. He was wearing gym clothes—nylon grey shorts with a neon orange stripe, a blue t-shirt, white socks, and sneakers—so I assumed he had gone to the gym before coming to work. Over the next few weeks I would realize how central his workout routine was to his life. He was a bit heavy, but I thought that perhaps if he ate less, he would have looked like a guy in one of his videos or maybe even one of those gym magazines. He certainly put the time in.

For lunch, he broke out some grilled salmon, fried chicken, and a protein shake. He was a loud eater, and we sat right next to each other. Slurping and sucking and chewing, with his headphones on, watching videos, Sital was oblivious to how those around him might react. I eventually got in the habit of leaving whenever he ate.

Perhaps worst of all, he often left food at his desk overnight, so the next morning the area would reek of day-old salmon.

I don't mean to be vicious. I realize that he was at the beginning of his career. And I'd bet that we all have the occasional unprofessional moment. Still, Sital had many such moments. These were my first impressions of him, and they became part of the calculus by which I judged Celolot's chances of success.

Eventually I decided to ask him about the video. I tapped his arm. He looked at me blankly. He took off his headphones.

"What are you watching?" I asked.

"Troy Adashun. Do you know him?"

"I don't. What's he all about?"

He looked at me intently. "Fast weight gain. He gained a lot of weight in one year."

"You mean muscle?"

"Yes. He gained a lot of muscle in one year."

"Ah." I thought I might break the ice with a joke about one of my own vices. "You know the brain contains approximately one hundred billion neurons? And only eight of mine function before I consume coffee?" I held up my empty cup of coffee. "I'm going to get some more. Do you want to come along?"

He just stared at me silently. Then he swiveled back to his screen. Two hours later, he was still watching videos about weightlifting.

I do get that everyone needs to take breaks. I sometimes check personal email at work; I sometimes stop and read *Hacker News*; I occasionally take a personal call. Overall, I have no objection to anyone checking on personal interests while at work. But if they're not getting their work done, then it's a pretty good indication that they need to cut back on the amount of weightlifting videos they're watching.

FRIDAY, MAY 29TH, 2015

Sital and I had to figure out what technologies we would use and how my software would talk to his software.

"What language are you thinking about using for this project?" I asked him.

"I know Python the best," he said.

"So you'll use Python?"

"No, I'm gonna use Java," he said. "It's supposed to be very powerful for NLP."

"Supposed to be?" I was wary of his uncertainty. "You aren't sure?"

"It's innovative," he said, somewhat vacantly.

"Innovative?" I wanted him to clarify his reasoning.

"How much can you lift?" he asked me.

"What?" I blinked. I thought I hadn't heard him correctly.

"How much can you bench press?"

Was he really asking me this? I collected my thoughts and decided he must have simply been changing the subject to something that interested him, since I had apparently been discussing an issue that bored him. I had no impression that he was engaging in any kind of machismo.

"Oh, I don't lift," I replied. "I run, but I don't lift."

"Do you know what your bone density is?" he asked.

"I guess not …" Now I was puzzled by the direction of the conversation.

"It's extremely important, you know," he said. "They've been finding that it's a leading health indicator for many other diseases."

"Osteoporosis?"

"That's the obvious one, but even stuff like heart disease and Alzheimer's."

"I wonder what the connection is," I remarked, sincerely interested for a moment.

"I don't know, but if you don't know your bone density, you could die suddenly, and you won't know why." He sounded extremely passionate.

"Well, that would be awful," I chuckled. "I'm sure I'd like to know why I'm dead."

"Most people would!" he concurred. "You need to get measured!"

"Uh, well … I've been meaning to, of course."

"When you lift weights, your bones become more dense," he went on.

"And when a person goes jogging?"

His countenance was incredibly serious. "I doubt it. I bet joggers die younger than weight lifters."

"But what about all the cardio benefits?" I felt the need to defend all joggers everywhere.

"Maybe," he conceded. "But you should measure. Go now. It's important."

"Right, absolutely." Then I cleared my throat. "So, um, about our software. You're thinking you'll use Java?"

"Oh, right. Yeah, totally. Yeah. It's so …"

"It's so?" I was still hoping he might be able to clarify the reasons for his strategy.

"It's so …" he trailed off.

"Innovative?" I thought he might finally say something if I reminded him where he'd paused the conversation earlier.

"Yes! Totally! That! We'll use Java!"

"Well. I'm glad we had this talk." I realized that I wasn't going to get any substantial discourse out of him.

"Just remember to measure your bone density," he concluded.

"I'll keep it in mind," I said, but I never did get my bone density checked.

There is something bittersweet about recalling first impressions. During my first few conversations with Sital I would have used four adjectives to describe him: quirky, friendly, honest, and innocent. He was twenty-three years old and had graduated from school a year ago. Then

15

he'd worked at Chase for a year, where he had used Python to generate revenue projections by building something like fancy spreadsheets and charts. That is a perfectly respectable first job, but we would eventually have to confront what it meant for us: he had never used GitHub, nor any other tool for collaborating with his coworkers, he had never worked with other computer programmers, and he had never used Java in a professional setting.

The skills he lacked were going to cost us a great deal of time.

MONDAY, JUNE 1ST, 2015

I had worked out the architecture that I wanted us to pursue. Since there were only four of us at Celolot, each of us had an undeniably important job. Hwan would build the iPhone app. Sital—since he was the NLP guy on our team—would build our NLP engine. I would build the API app that connected the iPhone app and the NLP engine. I would also build the Salesforce app, which would take the message from the NLP engine and send it to Salesforce. John would be our salesperson, lining up potential customers and getting them excited about the software we would soon be ready to show them.

With all that decided, John bought a train ticket for Hwan and put him up in a hotel in New York so the whole team could be together for two days.

John had hired a design company in Brooklyn to create the visuals for our iPhone app. We grabbed a conference room and reviewed them together. Hwan laughed when he saw it. The Brooklyn company had gone a bit wild being "innovative." They were not employing any of the standard user interface elements that Apple makes available to all iPhone developers. Hwan would have to write hundreds of custom widgets to implement the designs; the whole thing might take six months to a year to build.

John, on the other hand, thought the designs were really cool. "Oh, man, this is the best!" he exclaimed, with a grin plastered on his face.

For sure, they were full of eye candy. Aside from games, it was the most visually arresting iPhone app that I'd ever seen.

All software projects start with a wishlist of features, most of which never get built: dazzling animations, wild new features, alerts, sounds, new ways of storing data. John had spent months daydreaming about the kind of software that might totally reinvent the sales industry. But now that

16

we'd been hired and he had to pay us, it was time to focus on what would make money in the short term. Salespeople had told John they were desperate to find an easier way to record their Opportunities, so that would be our first goal. (Salesforce uses the word "Opportunity" to refer to any potential sale.) So the real question for us was, how long would that take? We all agreed it seemed like three months of work. If we stayed focused and pushed hard, we should have it done by August.

John encouraged us to pick titles for ourselves. Our only limit was we couldn't call ourselves the CTO. Anything else was fine. So Hwan chose the title of Lead Mobile Developer. Sital would be Lead Data Scientist. I would be Lead Engineer. We were oh-so-very proud of our superlative positions.

TUESDAY, JUNE 2ND, 2015

John took some time off from school to join us for part of the day.

Apparently Sital's lack of experience had been factored into the plans from the beginning. He would need some advice from a high-level NLP expert. Someone on our board of directors had recommended a guy named Arthur, who lived in Houston, Texas. John had arranged to fly Arthur to New York for four days. Celolot put him up at the nearby Marriott.

Arthur turned out to be a great guy with a combination of traits that are sadly rare. He was an absolute expert in his speciality, yet he had no ego about it. If we asked a question he couldn't answer, he never tried to bluff. Instead, he would very simply explain that he didn't know the answer, track down the information, and get back to us as soon as he could.

We spent much of the day in a conference room, discussing the NLP strategy that we would pursue. In particular, we had to figure out what level of accuracy we were comfortable with.

This is the current state of NLP: any idiot can write an NLP program that will correctly parse the meaning of a sentence 70% of the time. If you get together a team of PhDs and have them create some highly refined algorithm that is optimized for your particular case, then you can up that to 95%. The difference between 70% and 95% is the difference between what is cheap and what is expensive. There is no way to get 100% accuracy. Not even Google can guess your intentions 100% of the time.

Every professional software developer has to sometimes find patterns in text. We do this by using a technology known as "regular expressions," or regex for short. A universal skill, all programmers know it. But NLP is too complex for regex. Thankfully the government has subsidized research at universities to come up with something better, and Stanford University eventually developed a library of code known as the Stanford NLP library. It is free and open source, so most startups focused on NLP use the Stanford library. The library is rich with nuance, and we spent the day discussing what those nuances implied for our particular case.

Among our concerns, we had to counteract word associations that might embarrass us. Since we were relying on libraries of code that had been produced by other organizations, whose goals were sometimes at odds with our own, we'd need to be careful that their biases did not leak into our work.

A year later Katharine Jarmul would write a great deal about this,[3] focusing on Google's NLP software Word2Vec. Among the worrisome matches she found, typing in "immigrant" brought back "illegal immigrant;" "negroes" brought back suggestions including "blacks," "slaves," and the n-word; and "jews" brought back "kikes." No doubt people search for horrible things on Google, and arguably it is right for Google to accurately reflect the word associations that people make, but for us it would have been extremely embarrassing if we suggested "illegals" every time a salesperson wrote the word "Mexican."

THURSDAY, JUNE 4TH, 2015

Another day spent learning from Arthur.

In the evening, I confronted John with my doubts about our current approach. Why we were working with Sital and not Arthur? If we wanted to build cutting-edge technology that no one else had, wouldn't it make more sense to work with the guy who was the obvious expert instead of a beginner like Sital?

He laughed. "Arthur is waaaaaay too expensive for us. We could never afford him."

"But have you thought about the possibility that he's worth the extra

18

money?" I prompted. "What if Arthur can get this done in June, whereas Sital is still working on this in August, or even September?"

"Well, first of all, Sital doesn't need till September," John answered. "And the main thing is, we can't afford Arthur for three months."

"But what if we only need him for three weeks?"

"We need someone for three months," insisted John. "We have to have a data scientist on staff."

I thought perhaps my basic idea was not getting through: "But, what I'm saying is, what if Arthur were able to build a working prototype in a short amount of time?"

"We would still need to have him on staff."

"Why? Why would we need to have him on staff?"

"Reasons," said John, and he shrugged.

"Reasons?" I asked.

"Let's talk about it later."

I let it go, but the whole thing seemed suspicious.

FRIDAY, JUNE 5TH, 2015

I got to work at 9:30 A.M., which was early for me. I'd discovered a La Colombe a block away and it was my new favorite coffee place. After trying their Afrique brew I'd decided I'd never go to Starbucks again.

John was on another video call with Milburn. Since he was wearing headphones, I only heard half the conversation.

"Yeah … Yeah … Okay. I'll tell them. Yeah. I'll do it. I'm sorry. I didn't know. Yeah … I'll do it. I'm sorry."

I had to wonder if it was a bad sign that John was apologizing to a member of the board.

Even more odd: John was adding action items to PivotalTracker, the project management application we used to keep track of our tasks. But a board of directors is advisory, and board members typically only give high-level advice. Was Milburn dictating which tasks were priorities? That would be unusual.

Our final day with Arthur was spent in review. Did we have a coherent strategy? Did Sital feel he could act on it? Everything about this conversation made me nervous.

Sital assured us that he could pull it off. Arthur asked him what the plan was. Sital stalled and was unable to answer. I was reminded of the time when I was nine years old and my parents signed me up for swimming lessons, at the end of which I thought I was ready for the test, but in fact I nearly drowned.

Sital was a beginner. In general, there is nothing wrong with being a beginner. All of us are beginners at some point. And for the most part, I think corporations in the USA could do more to facilitate apprenticeships to help people start their careers. However, we were a startup that needed to move fast. Could we succeed when we had a beginner in a critical role? I had doubts.

Arthur left at 4:00 P.M., and Sital and John left shortly after that.

Varak and Perrino (the founder and CEO of EvenLife, which had started as a productivity app and then morphed into a startup focused on web server automation) were working late, and they ordered pizza. Then they started playing *League of Legends*. The atmosphere was festive. I stayed late just to hang out with the folks from the other startups.

SUNDAY, JUNE 7TH, 2015

Late at night, we were all working from our homes, and John posted to Slack (the chat software we used) that he had a potential customer lined up and needed to do a demo in a few days. Hwan explained that he would not have the iPhone app ready for testing until at least late July. John insisted that he only wanted to show the basics of how the NLP app parsed a sentence into fields such as "Product" and "Customer." I suggested we set up a simple website where a customer could type in a sentence and watch how our NLP software transformed it. However, I doubted that we could get it ready in a week. I was especially worried about Sital's work.

Just at that moment, Sital joined us on Slack. John asked him if he could have a working app by Wednesday. Sital said maybe. John insisted that it was important. Sital caved: sure, totally, absolutely.

I was worried that this was way too ambitious. I asked if we could have an additional week, just in case things did not go as expected. John challenged me: did we really need an extra week? I replied: we would look bad if we couldn't meet the deadline.

Fortunately, he agreed with me. He would schedule the demo for the seventeenth, and if it went well he could brag about it when he met with the board of directors on the eighteenth.

TUESDAY, JUNE 9TH, 2015

John told me that the board of directors had drawn up monthly sales goals for him. Starting in August, he would be expected to hit his quota. I thought this was insane. Once a product exists and is stable, then a company can draw up a sales schedule. How can one reasonably do that when the product does not even exist yet? Especially if the product is a cutting-edge technology which carries a lot of unknowns? For a stable company with an existing product, deadlines need to be more than mere aspirational goals, but when building truly original technology, then the entire company is aspirational—until the technology is working, there is no proof that the technology can work.

Even if the glorious day arrived when we would finally have an app customers could install on their iPhones, that would only be the beginning of a long process. Customers are an endless surprise. I've worked with start-ups for sixteen years; I know this well. Whenever I have shown people new software, the features that seemed intuitive to me were counterintuitive to them. Real-life needs that seemed intuitive to them seemed strange to me. If John thought that we could create our apps and have them working by mid-August, and he could immediately go out and start making tons of money, then he was sadly mistaken. If the board of directors thought that, then they were being badly misled.

John reminded us that he had a demo with a customer scheduled for the seventeenth and the board would be meeting on Thursday the eighteenth. It was important that he have some success to report. But the whole day went by and Sital had nothing to show me. Late that night I chatted with him on Slack.

lkrubner
@sital, if you can get me something on Thursday then John can test it on Friday. Otherwise, if you can get me something by Friday, then we can tell John to wait till Monday.

Sital
I'll let you know tonight how much I can get done

21

lkrubner
tell John, not me. He's the one who makes the schedule.

Sital
Ok, I'll send him an email

The next day John asked me if we were done. I assumed Sital never wrote him the email.

WEDNESDAY, JUNE 10TH, 2015

I was alone at the incubator. John was at school. Sital was not working today.

A gentleman in a suit sauntered around the incubator. I saw him talking with Varak for awhile. Later, he stopped by my desk. He seemed like a friendly guy, around the age of thirty, a bit overdressed for the incubator.

He introduced himself as Ali Hariri. He worked at a well-known venture capital firm out in Silicon Valley, but now he was scouting the burgeoning New York startup scene. We chatted for half an hour and he seemed sincerely interested in what we were up to.

He asked me how we planned to compete with Tactile.com. I had never heard of them. He warned me that he'd just spoken with the CEO at Tactile and they were considering something similar to our project.

After he left, I investigated Tactile. They'd launched in 2014. They'd raised almost $12 million. The founder and CEO was Chuck Ganapathi, who'd previously worked at Salesforce.[4] Their first app had been minor, but they had over ten thousand salespeople using it. And according to Hariri, they were considering using NLP to build a new interface for Salesforce.

So this was our competition: they had more money than us, more existing relationships with users, more experience with Salesforce, and probably a larger software development team. That didn't mean they would beat us, but it did mean we would have to be very smart if we were going to survive.

In his 1985 book, *Innovation and Entrepreneurship*, the great business guru Peter Drucker had written a warning, which very much applied to Celolot:

In the 1920s, literally hundreds of companies were making radio sets and hundreds more were going into radio stations. By 1935, the control of broadcast-

ing had moved into the hands of three "networks" and there were only a dozen manufacturers of radio sets left. Again, there was an explosion in the number of newspapers founded between 1880 and 1900. In fact, newspapers were among the "growth industries" of the time. Since World War I, the number of newspapers in every major country has been going downhill steadily. And the same is true of banking. After the founders—the Morgans, the Siemenses, the Shibusawas—there was an almost explosive growth of new banks in the United States as well as in Europe. But around 1890, only twenty years later, consolidation set in. Banking firms began to go out of business or to merge. By the end of World War II in every major country only a handful of banks were left that had more than local importance, whether as commercial or private banks. ... But each time without exception the survivor has been a company that was started during the early explosive period. After that period is over, entry into the industry is foreclosed for all practical purposes. There is a "window" of a few years during which a new venture must establish itself in any new knowledge-based industry.[5]

A window of a few years had recently begun during which the world would certainly see an explosion of businesses that used NLP in some fundamental way. And Celolot was on the cutting edge of this new era. Yet every day that passed we were closer to losing our opportunity.

SATURDAY, JUNE 13TH, 2015

I worked from home. I reviewed all of Sital's code and wrote a long email with sixteen suggestions. Later, on Slack, he replied that he would implement all of the suggestions by Monday. I found that doubtful. Some of my suggestions were quick fixes, but a few were long-term ideas.

SUNDAY, JUNE 14TH, 2015

Hwan contacted me on Slack. Would the software be ready for the demo that John had planned for the seventeenth? I was doubtful. Sital's code was full of bugs, and he was a novice of a computer programmer.

Frustrated, Hwan made several suggestions, and wondered why John and I were not doing more to help Sital. In fact, we were doing all we could.

Isolated in DC, Hwan couldn't tell if we were effective in moving the project forward. I realized it would be crucial for Hwan and me to spend more time face to face. I sent an email to John suggesting that once a week Celolot buy me an Amtrak ticket to Washington. John wrote back immediately to tell me we couldn't afford that.

What the hell? Three weeks ago we were asked to take a poll to decide if we should get a free cleaning service for our apartments or a free gym membership. Now we didn't have money for a train ticket?

I wrote back to him and pointed out that my ability to work directly with Hwan was crucial to the project, whereas a lot of the perks that had been discussed had absolutely nothing to do with it.

He replied that he would need to check with the board.

Like a student who waits all weekend and then tries to do their homework late on Sunday, Sital reached out to me on Slack around 7:00 P.M. He didn't understand the vast majority of what I'd emailed him the previous day. So I wrote him back, attempting to re-write my ideas using simple language. Some of my advice was so specific ("use a hashmap, not an array") that I could have more quickly gone into his code and made the change myself, but I thought it would be educational for him to do it. When I spoke of general computer science topics, I included links to articles which I thought he should read.

John emailed me just before 11:00 P.M. and informed me that I would be allowed to go to DC twice a month. I was willing to live with that. I also planned to go visit some old friends in Virginia, so I figured there would be some weeks I would stop through DC and just pay for it myself.

This was to become a pattern, where John would zigzag wildly from excessive generosity to excessive thrift. I assumed this was because of his inexperience as a CEO; he simply didn't know what expenditures should be prioritized.

By this point in my life, my tolerance for bad leadership was minimal. For six years, in Virginia, I worked with a business partner who had lacked the temperament to build a great enterprise. Sometimes I feel sorry for myself about the lost opportunities of those years, but mostly I consider them a learning experience: a startup needs smart and consistent leadership. I was ready to quit Celolot if it began to seem like another hopelessly misdirected venture.

But I was also willing to give John a chance. He was young and I was willing to believe that he was eager to learn how to build a business. We'd only been working together for three weeks. I was hoping that we could establish a relationship where he would realize the wisdom of accepting my advice. For instance, regarding Sital, either we would see improvement or we would need to fire him. So long as I could get John to see things my way, then I very much wanted to continue. The technology we were working on was brilliantly ambitious, so I loved this project.

WEDNESDAY, JUNE 17TH, 2015

The day arrived when John had promised to do a demo for our first potential customer. Their meeting was scheduled for the late afternoon. But as of that morning, Sital was still struggling to get his code to work.

Sadly, the slightest variation on any of our sample sentences broke all the "pattern matching" that Sital's code was trying to do.

So for instance, this worked:

Sheraton Hotels is buying one million bottles of shampoo for 500000. Close date is August 1st. We must deliver by September 1st.

and this worked:

Sheraton Hotels is buying 2 million bottles of shampoo for 500000. Close date is August 1st. We must deliver by September 1st.

but this did not:

Sheraton Hotels is buying two million bottles of shampoo for 500000. Close date is August 1st. We must deliver by September 1st.

It turned out that his code didn't recognize numbers when they were written out. Where it saw "million" and no other number, it would default to 1,000,000—so "one million" seemed to work, but that was an accident. His code *did* see actual numbers, so "2 million" was correctly understood as 2,000,000. But "two million" or "three million" or "four million" or "forty million" were all read as "million," which defaulted to "one million" and became 1,000,000.

By noon, Sital was finally able to find the number that modified "million," so now "two million" gave us 2,000,000, which was what we wanted. But John, testing this code, found that dollar signs broke everything:

> I just sold 1 million bottles of shampoo to Sheraton Hotels, revenue $500000. Contract August 1. Delivery September 1.

This gave us revenue of zero, and all the dates vanished.

```
Contact:
Customer: Sheraton Hotels
Product: Shampoo
Quantity: 1,000,000
Revenue: $0
Close Date:
Delivery Date:
Username:
Salesforce username:
```

When Sital's code encountered a dollar sign, it stopped reading the text completely. I thought that was suspicious. We had agreed to not use regex for this project because it added complexity and yet was not powerful enough to handle NLP. But a dollar sign has a special meaning in regex—and sure enough, when I looked at his code I saw that he had spent the last few days writing a tremendous amount of regex.

John tended to avoid direct confrontation, but he found ways to express his frustration. He would ask Sital if the code was ready, then ask again thirty minutes later, then ask again thirty minutes later, then ask again thirty minutes later. He would ask to see a sample of what was broken, and Sital would show him. John would shake his head and say something like, "We are losing money every minute this isn't working."

The more nervous Sital felt, the more he used regex. The Stanford library was overwhelming, and regex was something he understood. He needed the comfort of something familiar.

To my mind, this was exactly the same as being lost at sea, dying of thirst, and drinking the brine. It's a kind of suicide.

Some time in the early afternoon, John stood up, looked at Sital, and then sat down. He glanced at his computer screen, got up again, then sat down again. He ran his hand over his face. Then, erupting with frustration, he jumped up, turned around to face Sital and demanded, "I want this to work RIGHT NOW!"

"I know! I know!" cried Sital, who kept staring at his screen, looking terribly confused.

"Well, when will it be working?" asked John angrily.

"Um …" Sital had no answer. "Um …"

"God dammit!" shouted John. Then he stormed off and left the incubator.

Clearly, he would have to reschedule the demo. And he would have to go to the board of directors meeting tomorrow without having any notable success to brag about.

Despite all the painful delays, Sital was making progress. This was one of the rare nights when he worked late with me. We were getting closer and closer to the moment where a potential customer could test the code from our demo website. I could go to the site and type a sentence, hit the "Send" button, and the sentence went to my API app. If he could get his app working, and we could connect my API app to his NLP app, we would have something we could show the world.

How did he want to send messages back and forth between our apps? I was in favor of using "named pipes," a very old Unix technology, as a short-term solution that I thought could be implemented with seven or eight lines of code. But Sital knew nothing about named pipes, and he was overwhelmed by all the other technologies he still needed to learn.

Once panic starts, learning stops. Therefore I felt that one of the most important things we needed to do, as a team, was remove some of the pressure Sital was feeling. I decided I would let him make this decision. How did he want the two apps to talk to each other? We would do whatever he thought was easiest.

But he had absolutely no idea.

SUNDAY, JUNE 21ST, 2015

I spent the weekend drinking large amounts of coffee and working on the charts that helped make our demo website look dazzling. John was in love with these charts and decided they would be very important to selling the software. Any kind of eye candy appealed to him: bright colors, animations, sounds that imitated older analog technologies, like the sound of an old cash drawer opening; anything that looked like a video game.

I did not hear from Sital.

My friend Michael called me and asked me if I was doing anything that night. I told him I was working. He asked me how it was going. I thought about it and finally said the project was very exciting, though our execution so far left me deeply nervous about our chances of success.

That night John sent us all a message on Slack:

John
July 3rd. Very important posssble customer. Must be working. crucial.

Saturday, June 27th, 2015

Sital fixed the inconsistent appearance (or disappearance) of the dollar sign in the "Revenue" field, but his fix broke all the dates. Then he fixed the issue with the dates, but he did so by including a new library of code. This changed how the dates were formatted. "October 12th" became "10-12." I spent the morning rewriting the way the code on the demo site handled dates.

All of a sudden I felt intense disappointment with everything we had done so far. When I first heard of Celolot at the beginning of May, I had assumed that it was a company that would be using advanced algorithms to do sophisticated pattern matching on the sentences we were given. Instead, we were struggling to do the basics. So far our supposedly cutting-edge NLP algorithms consisted of the sample code that came with the official documentation of the Stanford NLP library. Sital had literally copy-and-pasted the code and then made minor adjustments to get it to work for our circumstances. I could have easily done everything that he had so far done.

More so, there was no possibility of us doing things The Right Way. The year before I'd written a popular essay titled "Object Oriented Programming Is An Expensive Disaster Which Must End,"[6] which was thirty thousand words of me explaining how to create good, reliable code. I'd argued in favor of the new Functional style, rather than the old Object Oriented style. But Sital barely understood the old style and seemed to have no interest in learning the new style.

This was the price we were paying for the long hours that he spent watching videos on YouTube. Those were hours that Sital could have spent learning more about computer programming. I had to wonder how differently this month would have gone if we had fired Sital and hired Arthur full time.

But I wasn't angry with Sital. I was angry with John, for playing what seemed like a losing strategy, and for being stubborn about it.

Would we be ready for the big demo on July 3rd? I had no confidence.

In the afternoon, I rented a car and drove to Charlottesville, Virginia. I had lived in Charlottesville for nine years and still had many friends down there. I was excited to see them and to get away from the drama of Celolot for a weekend.

Sunday, June 28th, 2015

Among other things, I was working on a series of essays about computer programming which I planned to eventually turn into a book. My good friend Natalie was helping me edit them. Her schedule had opened up and she arranged to come visit me for two weeks, so I drove from Charlottesville to Virginia Beach to get her, and then we drove back to New York.

During her stay, Natalie got to know the crew at Celolot, and her opinions became a healthy reality check for me. More so, I got in the habit of texting her bits of dialogue, especially after conversations which I thought were especially bizarre. These text messages later became the basis from which I recreated much of the dialogue in this book.

Monday, June 29th, 2015

Natalie came with me to work. The startup incubator had dozens of guests every day, so she blended right in. She sat on one of the couches and edited my essays. She didn't bother anyone, and no one bothered her.

I jumped right back in to where I had left off on Saturday. At some point I picked up my coffee and meandered toward the couches to see how she was doing. She handed me her edits to read, and I sat on the couch while she walked over to where Sital was watching a video about weightlifting.

Curious, Natalie asked about his interest in weight training. Sital, caught off guard, stuttered for a moment, then launched into a monologue: the link between protein and muscle mass, the importance of a high-protein diet, the dangers of carbohydrates. He talked about the various techniques that people used to measure bone density and how to determine the percentage of weight gain composed of bone versus the percentage composed of muscle. She thanked him for the lesson and rejoined me on the couch.

"If I ever need to gain a lot of weight fast, now I know how," she joked.

But the day was not funny. We had made zero progress on important issues such as how the NLP software would communicate with the API software. I had told Sital we could handle this however he thought easiest, but he had not had time to think about it, as he'd been distracted by the issue of dates and dollar signs and the damage caused by his use of regex.

Sital and I had a long talk about what might allow us all to go faster. The only decision we reached is that he would stop using the Microsoft Windows operating system and instead switch to a machine that ran Linux, which was the same software that ran on our servers. At least then there would be fewer surprises when he uploaded his software to the server. If he created the NLP software on a machine that ran Linux, then it should run on our server, which also used Linux.

For a few hours in the afternoon it seemed like we were making progress. But then John found that Sital had somehow broken all of the dates again. So Sital went back to looking at the code that was supposed to parse the dates. There was something pathetic about the way John pouted with anger yet did nothing to improve the situation.

Right across the street from the incubator is the New York City Fire Museum. The building itself is a renovated 1904 fire house which once housed FDNY Engine Company No. 30. It currently holds over ten thousand photographs, historical objects, and equipment highlighting and commemorating the service of the NY Fire Department.

Around 4:30 P.M., Natalie and I walked out of the incubator to go get lunch, but almost immediately we encountered a substantial commotion. A mix of spectators and firemen blocked the street. The firemen were in full uniform, standing around a vehicle, dousing it with blasts of water from their industrial hoses.

"Cool! Looks like they're doing a demonstration or reenactment for the museum," Natalie effused. As an artist, she was constantly photographing things which interested her. "I wanna get closer so I can take some pics."

But the shattered glass and smoking oil and awful stench of burning rubber all seemed a tad too convincing for a reenactment. Natalie, never having the slightest trepidation about asking questions, bounded up to one of the fire fighters and asked him, "Pardon me, um, sir? You look really busy but I'd like to know, are you and your coworkers providing a demo for museum attendees this afternoon?"

"No, ma'am," the fireman told her, respectfully but clearly serious. "This Jag was just rollin' along when the engine burst into flames."

It was a 1960 Jaguar MKII Saloon, jet black, and among the other alphanumerics, its license plate contained the notorious 666.

What should we say about circumstances that seem too absurd to be true? Right in front of the Fire Museum, a 1960 Jaguar with a 666 on its license plate spontaneously burst into flames. The surreal quality of that coincidence struck me as a metaphor for the way Celolot was failing.

Thursday, July 2nd, 2015

Natalie and I got to the office at 10:30 A.M. Sital arrived at 11:00. John was already there, quiet and brooding. He stared at his screen. He did not look at us. It seemed like he was afraid that if he opened his mouth, something confrontational would come out, and he hated confrontation.

We were aware that we had twenty-three hours left until his big demo with the potential customer.

On the one hand, I wanted Celolot to be successful and I wanted us to line up some customers, so I was ready to do everything in my power to make sure the demo went well. On the other hand, it was hard to feel much sympathy for John, since our delays were largely a self-inflicted wound. It had been obvious for weeks that Sital was slowing us down, but John hadn't even spoken to him about the long hours he spent watching weightlifting videos.

I had some minor work left to make the demo website look polished, but nothing urgent. Sital announced that his app was working, then he changed his mind and asked for another hour. I asked him if he needed my help but he repeated he only needed another hour. Natalie sat on one of the couches in the office to sketch—among her other talents, she was also a freelance artist and had recently gotten a commission to paint a mural at a restaurant.

Sital announced that his software was ready. He compiled it and we uploaded it to the server. We tested with this sentence:

Spoke to Carol. I just sold 1 million bottles of shampoo to Sheraton Hotels, rev 500000. Contract August 1. Delivery September 1.

Everything worked great. We tried a variation:

31

Spoke to Carol. I just sold 1 million bottles of shampoo to Sheraton Hotels. Total of $500000. Contract August 1. Delivery September 1.

That still worked great. Then we tried removing the periods:

Spoke to Carol I just sold 1 million bottles of shampoo to Sheraton Hotels Total of $500000 Contract August 1 Delivery September 1

Broken! We got the wrong delivery date and no close date at all.

Sital timidly suggested he would need another hour to fix the problem. I assumed that meant he would need another two hours. I asked if he needed help, but he downplayed it. I think he wanted to feel that he understood his code before he invited me to read it.

I worked on my side of the demo for two hours. To get ahead of possible problems, I wrote out the code he would need to use to connect to my app, and I emailed it to him.

At one point I leaned back to consider what difficulties we might face, put my hands in my pockets, stared hard at the screen, and was startled to feel a wet tongue on my skin. I looked down. A poodle with hopeful eyes was looking up. It wagged its tail. It sniffed my jeans. Lots of people brought their dogs to work. This one was very cute. I held up my hands to show it that I had no food. It continued to wag its tail, no doubt hoping that its big, sad eyes would melt my apparently cold, cruel heart. I rubbed its head. Finally it gave up on me, and went off looking for someone who might be more generous with snacks.

Sital was still not ready to talk to me. At 4:30 P.M. Natalie and I went out to lunch. I was mostly killing time until Sital was ready to talk to me. Natalie wanted to try Rockin Raw, a vegan restaurant. We arrived long before the dinner rush, so the place was empty except for a young woman from Norway. We struck up a conversation, first about raw foodists and then about Norway, and after a few minutes we invited her to join us. The fare was delicious and the conversation fascinating. It was a pleasant interlude, especially compared to how the evening would unfold back at the incubator.

When I returned, Sital quietly murmured that he was probably ready to test the communication between our apps.

It was 7:00 P.M.

We uploaded the software to the server and tried to send a message from one app to the other, using named pipes. That did not work, but we got no error message, which was surprising. Error messages are standard when code malfunctions.

"Where are the error messages?" I asked.

"I turned them off," replied Sital casually.

"Why would you do that?" I asked him. I was at a loss.

"They were confusing me," he said simply.

"Let's add some error messages."

"Where should we put them?"

"Around the code that reads and writes data to the named pipes," I instructed.

"What sort of error messages?"

I pulled my chair up to his desk so I could better see his screen. "Start with something general," I provided. "Catch any error."

That was the beginning of a very long slog. Had I known what we were facing, we might have done things differently. It became amazingly apparent that Sital had not yet installed all the software necessary for professional computer programming, even though he had been working at Celolot for eight weeks and had supposedly been working full time for three. He had installed none of the software that would let him test his own software, and he was still using Microsoft Windows even though he had promised to switch over to using Linux.

We fell into a painful repeating groove on the proverbial broken record. He would make a minor change to his code, then compile and upload it; I would test it; we would see an error, look for it, and spot it; then he would have to make another minor change. The whole cycle took about eight minutes per error.

Often the problem was something very minor, like missing a semicolon. That was eight minutes to type a semicolon. If he had been properly set up to test his code directly on his laptop, the whole cycle of find-a-bug, fix-the-bug, compile, retest would have taken one or two minutes. That six or seven minute difference didn't seem very significant the first two or three times we stumbled our way through it, but once we had gone through the cycle twenty times, I was livid.

Equally annoying was how he spent those minutes: he watched videos about weightlifting. He could have been studying named pipes since his lack of knowledge was precisely what was causing this delay, but instead he treated those minutes as a kind of break time.

It was 8:00 P.M. His app kept dying without telling us why. I was leaning over his shoulder now and advising him: "Put an error message on this line, and an error message on this line, and an error message on this line." The idea was to get his app to report its status on nearly every line so we could better understand where the problem was. Even under the best of circumstances, this kind of debugging is tedious. Given our eight-minute cycle time, it was downright excruciating, and we made only modest progress as the hours marched by.

At 9:00 P.M. the error reports made me realize that he had again confused the two different ways that Java dealt with directories—a mistake he would still be making even months later. This was part of the price Celolot had to pay because he had never used Java in a professional setting before.

By 10:00 P.M. the apps were able to send one message to each other, but not a second message.

The incubator was slowly emptying out. Natalie became restless. In our decade-long friendship, she has often remarked that her ADHD keeps her from being able to sit in one place very long. But in this case, she had simply not realized we'd be working so late.

She pulled me aside. "I'm too tired to do any more sketching."

"Why don't you go home?" I suggested. "You have a key."

"Will you be done soon?" she asked. "I'd be happy to wait for you if you'll be done soon."

I looked over my shoulder at Sital. "I wish I knew. At the rate we are going, it could easily be another hour or two."

"Another hour or two, really?"

"I'm afraid so."

She headed home and I went back to working with Sital.

By 11:00 P.M. we had figured out which part of the code threw an error when we tried to send a second message.

At this point Sital became extremely frustrated and insisted that we stop using named pipes. UNIX technology had come a long way in the last thirty years, he said, so there was no reason to use anything so old.

If I were dealing with an experienced programmer, we would be having a very different kind of conversation. There were dozens of great technologies that we could be using, but I was in a position where I felt I had to dumb things down to a level Sital could understand. So I asked him what he wanted to do.

"Let's use WebSockets!" he emoted. "They are really, really easy. I mean, it's ridiculous how easy they are. We wouldn't have any of these problems if we had just started with WebSockets and used them for everything."

That was a surprisingly strong endorsement, especially since he had never mentioned the WebSocket protocol before. Now he sounded as if he'd been wanting to use it from the beginning and I had been holding him back. If he'd simply started the evening by saying "I prefer to use WebSockets for this task," then I would have been happy to go along with him.

"Okay," I cautiously agreed. "If WebSockets will be easy for you, we can use those. How do you want to implement them?"

"Isn't there some library we can use?" he asked.

"There are probably dozens, if not hundreds."

"Okay, well, let me look."

We took a half an hour to read about some of the many WebSocket libraries. I would have to implement WebSockets in my app, and he would

34

have to implement them in his NLP app. Both apps would have to use the same technology so that they could talk to each other. This meant that I was studying WebSocket libraries in Clojure, whereas he was studying WebSocket libraries in Java. (Clojure is another programming language, one which I had found to be remarkably expressive and flexible.)

After thirty minutes I turned to him and said, "Well, to keep it simple, my app will make available a single endpoint. And you, too, should implement a single endpoint, and that's what I will call when I send a message to you."

"What is the end point?" he asked.

"Um, you know, the URL. The address we call to reach the other app."

"How do I implement a URL?"

"I don't know, I haven't been reading about the Java libraries. I've been reading about the Clojure ones."

"Oh." He fell silent for a bit and kept reading the documentation he had found for some library that he must have felt was a possibility for us.

I started working on implementing the WebSocket protocol. I had never worked with WebSockets before, so I had to read the documentation several times to figure out how I was supposed to implement them.

At midnight, he mumbled to me, "I don't get this. Do we have a web server?"

"Yes," I answered. I sat up a little straighter. "Why? Do you want me to set an alias for whatever URL you want to use as your endpoint? I could set up a reverse proxy."

"I think I need a web server to specify an endpoint."

"In your app, yes," I agreed. "Obviously you need something to listen for HTTP."

"How do I do that?"

"Well, how did you do it last time?"

"I've never done this before."

"You've never done this before?" I echoed in disbelief.

"No."

"Then why did you say it would be easy?"

"Well I've *read* that WebSockets are easy. Every time I read about them, they say it's easy. They're supposed to be easy."

"For God's sake, *every* technology is confusing the first time you work with it!"

"I just didn't know it would be this hard! They say it's easy!"

I didn't respond. I decided that I needed a break, preferably outside. I went downstairs to the street. The night was blazing hot and the air thick with the dense humidity of a summer heat wave that had gone too long without a major storm. Across the street was Essen, a cafeteria-style eatery that was open twenty-four hours and was very much loved by all of us who

35

worked late. Though bedlam during the day, at this hour the place offered a clean and quiet sanctuary away from work.

I bought a coffee and sat at one of the tables. One of the staff was mopping the floor. Two women came in, dressed in stylish office attire. I guessed they were in their mid-twenties. I wondered what they were working on at this hour. This neighborhood was several blocks away from any of the party scenes, so the only people who came into this Essen at this hour would be people working late, not people on their way home from something fun.

Finally I gathered myself and went back across the street to the incubator.

Sital had gone back to watching weightlifting videos.

"So did you decide what you want to do?" I asked calmly, even though I was furious.

He looked at me. "Oh! Well um … I think WebSockets are too complicated."

"Awesome. And did you decide what you want to do?"

"Well, what do you want to do?"

"I think we were making progress with named pipes."

He looked like I had kicked him. "I don't want to work with named pipes."

"Well then, what do you want to do?" I asked.

"Isn't there some technology we can use that's simple?" he asked meekly.

"There are a million technologies that we can use to send messages between two apps that live on the same server, but I'm not sure which technology you would consider simple."

"Why don't we use Redis?" he asked. Redis was yet another open-source software project we could employ.

"Well, I have thought of that."

"So?"

"Okay, we can give that a try." I felt like I was trying to humor a child who had become cranky while traveling through a strange and alien land. "I would need to install and configure it. That might take an hour. Do you think you can have your app ready to talk to Redis in an hour?"

"How do I get my app to talk to Redis?" he asked, looking frightened.

"I don't know!" I was at the limits of my patience. "You would find some library that talks to Redis, and you would include the library in your app. Then you would follow whatever instructions are given in the official documentation for that library. Can you find a good Java library that talks to Redis?"

"I guess so."

"You guess so?"

"I guess."

"I would like you to commit to making something work." I would have

36

really liked him to take some responsibility for getting his software into working order, but my genie lamp was fresh out of wishes.

"Well, how hard is Redis?" he asked.

"I think it is easy, but I don't know how hard it will be for you."

"Is it like WebSockets?"

"I bet that WebSockets are easy if you've worked with them before and confusing if you're working with them for the first time. And I think you'll find that Redis is exactly the same."

"Okay, okay, okay, okay!" he conceded. "We'll use Redis."

"That's fine." I accepted his concession calmly. "I am happy to install and configure Redis. But I don't want us having this same conversation an hour from now, you understand? I don't want you to tell me that Redis is too hard so we have to try some other thing."

"Yeah, okay."

I was so in need of a commitment from him on this decision that I deliberately used redundancy. I looked at him intently and again asked, "So you're agreeing that we're going to start using Redis, and we'll stick with it until we have it working?"

He kind of stared off for a moment. Then he proposed in a low volume, "Maybe we should just use named pipes …"

"Are you serious?"

"Yeah. Yeah, I think it would be easier to just use named pipes."

"Are you serious?" I repeated, this time out of sheer incredulousness.

"Yes."

Was I Jim Carrey, and was this *The Truman Show*? This entire night was feeling surreal.

"But you've hated them so far!" I asserted.

"Well, do you think we were making progress?" he asked.

"Yes, I do."

"Okay, so let's just use named pipes."

"Great!" I was so overwhelmed with the futility of trying to meet a deadline while tutoring a raw beginner that I managed to sound both sarcastic and serious. "I love that idea. Let's make them work."

So we went back to named pipes. It was 1:00 A.M. and we had just wasted two hours on a long excursion into researching other technologies.

We went back to dealing with the painful eight-minute cycle. I generally spent this time researching similar problems; Sital went right back to watching videos. This time they were about video games, à la PewDiePie.

At one point I snapped a photo of him. The game was something similar to Mario Brothers, and the colorful graphics were clear on his computer screen. He was sitting there laughing. I sent the picture to John. If I later lost my temper, I wanted John to understand why.

By 2:00 A.M. we had realized his app was dying for several reasons. The bug was tricky to solve because there were many bugs that all occurred on the same line. He was generating blank data (a null value) and then trying to write it to the named pipe, so it looked as if the problem was with the named pipe but really it was much deeper. His code was also repeatedly connecting to the named pipe instead of setting up the connection once, when the app was first started.

The crew at RavenCart were often the last ones to leave, but this particular night we outlasted them. At 3:00 A.M. Vladimir, the CTO, announced he was going home. The other four programmers on his team all followed suit. They staggered up, wearily collected their things, and nodded to us as they left. After that, Sital and I were alone at the incubator.

By 4:00 A.M. we had his app connecting to the named pipe correctly.

By 5:00 A.M. we had achieved the big breakthrough: our apps could now send messages back and forth freely. There was only one remaining issue, which was that we had to figure out how to know when a message had been fully delivered. Had I been working with an experienced programmer, we would have simply used a library to handle this part of the work for us. With Sital, I was uncertain about what constituted "easy." He often seemed confused when he had to import a new library. But writing our own deserialization code seemed like an extremely tedious undertaking.

When I first suggested that we use a library to convert our data, Sital complained that I was making things unnecessarily complicated. Oddly insistent, he began to write code to serialize and deserialize his data. Of course, he had never tried something like this before and had no idea what sort of minefield he was stepping into. I decided to give him an hour to try things his way.

By 6:00 A.M. he had fully realized how tedious the task would be. Still, he was terrified of introducing a new library. We only had four hours left before John needed to do his demo for the big potential customer. Sital did not want us to get into another situation where we wasted two hours on a failed experiment, as we had with WebSockets, so he decided to keep hacking on the approach that he'd already started on. I gave him advice, even though I knew it was a doomed effort.

The cleaning crew came through. They were loud for fifteen minutes as they gathered up all the garbage, and then they left.

At 7:00 A.M. the lead engineer at Voice of Law came in. Over the next few months, as I stayed at the incubator many nights, I learned that he almost always came in that early.

Exasperated, Sital admitted we should use a library of code to handle the conversion of his data. Thankfully this went well: in thirty minutes we found a library, installed it, and had it working.

By 8:00 A.M. we were able to send messages back and forth between the apps, and the apps were able to convert all the characters. Then he discovered yet another bug in the way his app parsed sentences, which he had to fix, and in fixing this he changed the way he sent data back to my API app.

It was now 8:30 A.M. and Sital was done with his side of things, but I still had to update the demo website with the changes that he had just made.

I was feeling tired, but I thought I might be able to keep going with more coffee. And perhaps a walk would wake me up.

The incubator didn't usually fill up till 10 A.M., but by 8:30 there were perhaps a dozen people in the room. It was beginning to feel like an office.

Sital was tired and wanted to go home. I said I would walk out with him. He seemed very worried about the deadline. We only had ninety minutes left. Would I be able to update the website in time? I told him I would try.

We headed out. I took the subway up to Ninety-Sixth Street, found a coffee shop, and got to work.

It was 9:00 A.M. I opened my computer and dove into the code. I had an hour left before the demo. Sital had changed the way the dates and numbers were formatted, so I had to adjust all the charts to make sure they understood the format of the data they were supposed to reflect.

I worked until 9:45. John was supposed to do the demo at 10:00. He messaged me on Slack.

John
Are you don yt? What are status?

lkrubner
The fields from the sentence render, but all the charts are broken. You can see the "Product" and "Customer" and "Revenue" fields, and we get the right data, but I need another two hours to redo the charts. Do you want to do the demo without the charts? Just show how the sentence renders?

John
Damn

Fifteen minutes later, just after 10 A.M., I was anxious to hear how it was going.

lkrubner
Are you doing the demo now?

John
dem cancellled.

39

I called it quits and went back to the apartment. Natalie had made herself breakfast and was sipping tea. She laughed when I came in. I thought about laughing but then decided against it. I was too tired.

I told her I had to get some sleep. She went out to explore the city on her own. I slept for ten hours and then joined her in the evening for a late dinner. Although fireworks are illegal in the city, someone set off Roman candles that burst huge in the sky. The country was getting ready to celebrate Independence Day.

I felt no sympathy for John. Hiring Sital had been his call, as was failing to hire Arthur. These last few weeks had offered plenty of evidence that Sital was a liability to the team. If John wanted to stick with Sital, he would have to live with the consequences.

I would feel very differently if Celolot had a formal commitment to an apprenticeship program, and if I had clearly been given the responsibility of running that program. But it was ridiculous to both want to run an aggressive schedule and also train a beginner. The one contradicts the other.

TUESDAY, JULY 7TH, 2015

Early in the morning I got a call from Mera, the woman at the talent agency who had first connected me with Celolot. Was I free for lunch? She indicated the subject was pretty urgent. I met her at her office, and she took me to a bar she loved in SoHo.

"Try the grapefruit margaritas," she said with exaggerated enthusiasm. "I love them!"

We both got grapefruit margaritas.

"What's up?" I asked tentatively. I really wasn't sure what to expect from this rendezvous.

"How are things going over there?" she asked, sipping from her glass.

"Not great. I could bore you with the details, but you said something was urgent?"

Mera pulled no punches. "John called us. He is very frustrated with the situation."

I already knew that John disliked direct confrontation, but I was amazed that he was so frightened by it that he would rather have a talent agency talk to me than talk to me himself.

"I'm frustrated with the situation, too," I said.

"Great, then you have common ground."

"Obviously we have common ground. We're both trying to build this startup."

"See?" She was pleased. "So there is no reason for you to fight." She smiled contently and sat back in her chair, as if she were trying to convince herself that it was all resolved now. She brushed a strand of hair away from her face and took another sip.

"John and I have never fought." I wanted to make sure she knew this.

"But he is frustrated, as I said."

"What did you hear exactly?"

"That there were delays."

I didn't think it was appropriate for me to list all of my grievances with Sital to someone who was outside of the firm, so I remained silent about our twenty-three hour marathon from July 2 into July 3. Still, I had to wonder what John thought had occurred that night. Did he think I was responsible for the delays we'd been suffering?

"I don't want to get into the details," I said somewhat guardedly. "But I think John knows why I'm aggravated."

"Well, what should I say?" Now she seemed genuinely worried. "I need to explain the situation to him."

Resurrecting my earlier line of thought, it occurred to me that I was in the middle of a very silly conversation. Whatever needed to be said between me and John should in fact be said while John and I were in a room alone together. The notion that John and I might communicate by passing messages through the talent agency which had hired me was possibly the single most ridiculous idea that I was to encounter during the entire year of 2015. This conversation, over grapefruit margaritas with Mera, was an insane way to clear up communication among the team.

All the same, her firm was paying for lunch, so we ordered another round. If John had set up this meeting, then I was entirely justified in drinking all day. And for Mera, getting drunk with people was part of her profession. Our food came, and for a little while we chatted about the weather and other insignificant things.

Finally I came up with an analogy in order to address her question. "It's like a basketball team," I said. "Or any sports team. It takes time to gel. I believe this team has potential, but we need to figure out a way to work effectively."

"I think that is very true," she said. Then she asked, "Do you think the team would be more effective if you brought in someone else?"

Of course, her income depended on firms such as ours hiring more people, so she was hungry for the chance to show us some candidates. She got a commission on every programmer who we hired.

"Possibly," I hedged, "but I think we need to work through some of our current communication issues before we make our next hire."

"Well, will you let me know when you're ready to think about your next hire?"

"Of course."

About an hour later I staggered out of there and took a taxi to the incubator. And for once, I was just as productive as Sital.

WEDNESDAY, JULY 8TH, 2015

Oddly enough, John was at the office when I got there.

"Aren't you supposed to be at school?" I asked him.

He shrugged. "I stopped going."

I laughed. "Do your parents know?"

"Not yet."

I was pleased. Now he could work as much as the rest of us.

I told him I wanted to discuss Sital, so we went to a conference room where we could have a private conversation.

"You realize that we are running a week or two late because of Sital?" I asked.

"I think we had some issues that we had to work through."

"Does our speed worry you?"

"I want us to go fast with the resources that we have."

I very much wanted him to consider the alternate reality where we had chosen to work with real talent. "Have you thought about where we might be right now if we had hired Arthur instead?"

"It doesn't matter, because Hwan still needs a few more weeks." He sounded a bit defensive. "And Sital, well, he's a junior programmer, and he accepted a salary on that basis. He's, uh, you know. He … isn't very expensive."

"If he slows us down, then he's actually very expensive."

"He hasn't really slowed us down." John was still sounding defensive. "Hwan still needs more time. Everything is on track for August."

I found it strange that he was frustrated enough to ask Mera to talk to me, but now that he and I were talking face to face, he acted as if we were running the Platonic Ideal of a startup. I assumed this was due to his intense dislike of confrontation.

I leaned toward him. "But what happens after we launch? Our customers will give us feedback. They will want features that we have not even thought of. What happens then? What happens when it's September or October or November and we are still moving slowly because of Sital?"

John laughed and stood up. "Well, that's not gonna happen! He'll get better. And anyway, by then we'll have enough money that we can hire a whole team of NLP experts!"

"What if we don't have as much money as you assume?"

"Are you kidding? We've got so much money coming our way that we don't have to worry," he repeated excitedly. "Pretty soon we can hire a whole army of NLP programmers!"

"Are you sure about this?"

"I'm one hundred percent sure! Don't worry! This is a lock."

But I wasn't so certain. My experience with startups had taught me that you never have money until it's actually in your bank account. One of your investors might be a good friend of yours and might swear on their mother's grave that they're going to send you money, and it still wouldn't mean a thing. I've even had customers tell me they'd waited their whole lives for my software, and I walked away from those conversations certain they were going to buy—yet they never did. Deals can fall apart at the last minute. You can never be sure.

More so, I was nervous about his apparent swing from pessimism to optimism. For six years I had to deal with the wild swings in my ex–business partner's moods, and I would hate to again be dealing with someone who exhibited the same issue. It's like dealing with the weather in London: you leave home and it's a sunny day, an hour later it's raining and bitterly cold, an hour after that it's sunny but windy, an hour later it's foggy but calm. When you're business with a person like that, you learn that no conversation can ever lead to an agreement that lasts more than a few days.

I wish I could say that the chaotic leadership at Celelot was unique, but in fact it's been the norm at most of the startups where I've worked. Good leadership is rare. Many entrepreneurs consider themselves free spirits who shouldn't be caged by a corporate hierarchy, and many come from wealthy backgrounds so they've never had to engage in work that they did not enjoy. Such people become entrepreneurs primarily because they think entrepreneurship will be fun. This is not conducive to professionalism.

An English language interface for a CRM was a brilliant idea. I loved the ambition of the project. But I was aware the leadership situation would either need to evolve quickly, or the project would fail.

Thursday, July 9th, 2015

Natalie took off on her own adventures in the city. Raw food was a new kick she was into, and her research lead her to Quintessence, on East Tenth Street, which became one of our favorite places. Among other creations, they had a dessert which they called the Coconut Banana Creme Pie, which was amazing. Sometimes we would order three slices and split the last one.

Natalie and I arranged that I'd catch up with her for a late lunch, at Quintessence or elsewhere.

Back at Celolot, we finally had a working system where a message from the web could arrive at our API app, the API app would send it to the NLP app, the NLP app would parse it and send it back to the API app, and the API app could send the result to whoever had sent the original message. It would be another month before Hwan had the iPhone app working, but John very much wanted to demo the software. To his credit, John was willing to work very hard at making sales. He lined up dozens of meetings with potential customers.

Responses were very positive. Several companies suggested they would be interested in using our software as soon as it was done. Of course, that raised the question of what they thought "done" meant. Doing a demo that gets potential customers to say, "That is so cool!" is rather easy. Getting them to actually give you money is difficult.

All the same, a wave of euphoria swept over John, which he communicated to the board of directors. Much later, I learned that at this time they began to schedule their plans around the assumption that we'd be making significant money by September. Again, though I can admire a sales team that aims to hit aggressive targets, making such plans around a product that doesn't yet exist, and which seems to be running behind schedule, is delusional.

Twice a month the incubator threw a "Whiskey Wednesday," and all of us oddballs and visionaries knocked back some bourbon and bragged about whatever we were working on. Natalie and I sat on a long couch and spoke with Niklas, Daniel, and Svetlana, who were from Sweden, Australia, and Russia, respectively. They were working together in a startup called Some Scenes Seen. Old journalism was dead, shouted Niklas, who'd already had too much to drink. Power corrupts! he added, spit flying as he yelled; the old media elites were decadent and needed to be overthrown by young visionaries such as himself. Svetlana optimistically offered that they were hoping to reinvent journalism via a focus on being hyper-local. Daniel, either more sane or more sober than Niklas, lucidly explained that they were trying to build an auction mechanism for creating certain kinds of video stories on tight deadlines.

Startups are a hellish grind, except when they're a party, and the incubator offered a fantastic place for those of us foolish enough to dare to build something entirely new.

SATURDAY, JULY 11TH, 2015

I drove Natalie back to Virginia Beach. We laughed about all the people she'd met at the incubator.

The drive isn't terrible, but it's still pretty substantial—close to eight hours. In addition to talking with me, Natalie pulled up all kinds of articles on her iPad to read.

"Oooh, Lawrence!" Natalie trilled. "It says, 'Chronic low-dose exposure to coffee is known to reduce the risk of certain cancers by a mechanism that is not understood.' So it looks like you have a much lower risk of getting cancer!"

"But Nat, it's not 'low-dose'—it's extremely high-dose. Does that have the same effect?"

"I'm not sure." She strove to find the answer, but apparently little research has been done regarding the health benefits of drinking two pots of coffee a day.

After I dropped her off, I drove up to Charlottesville.

MONDAY, JULY 13TH, 2015

I left Charlottesville and drove to Washington, DC I dropped off my rented car, then went over to the WeWork co-working space where we rented a space for Hwan.

Hwan and I grabbed a conference room and connected with John and Sital via video. Hwan was able to show us the various screens he had built on the iPhone which would allow salespeople to create and edit their Opportunities and Tasks (another Salesforce term). He was making significant progress, especially considering all the special custom widgets he was being asked to build.

Sital had made some progress, but then his app had stopped working. We all agreed that stabilizing the NLP app was a serious issue. I said I would work on it.

Three times John interrupted to say that we needed to start making money soon.

After our meeting, Hwan and I went to get a late lunch. Both of us had noticed John's paranoia about income. His recent vacillation between euphoria and panic struck us as nearly schizophrenic. Did Celolot really have $1.3 million dollars? Perhaps the money was promised to them only if they hit certain benchmarks and we were failing to hit those benchmarks? Hwan wondered what would happen to the company if we were not making money by September. I told him that I was concerned, too.

We worked until 7:00 P.M. and then I got a train to New York. I got back to my apartment at 1:00 A.M. I lay awake for awhile and tried to guess what was really happening—was the board of directors putting unnecessary pressure on John, or were we actually out of money?

John's fear reminded me of the disquiet which my partners and I had known during much of the era from 2002 to 2008. I could say that we burned through $3 million over the course of six years, but that doesn't communicate the stop-and-go nature of that time period. When we were running low on money, I'd go off and freelance until we had enough to make another go of it. Gallows humor got us through. I couldn't imagine John engaging in such humor.

Actually, I couldn't imagine John engaging in any kind of humor. He had only two modes: the superficial, carefree tone that he used with most people, which seemed to grow out of an insipid desire to please, and a terrified frenzy that he exhibited whenever he heard bad news.

From back in the era of my venture in Charlottesville, I can recall a dialogue I had with my friend Michael. It was around the summer of 2006. My business partner and I had run out of money again, but more seriously than ever before. It didn't look like we'd recover.

Michael had been working closely with us, so he was intimately aware of the financial terrain we were facing. He was one of the most cynical people I'd ever known, which was why I liked him. One night we decided to go out for drinks and verbally assess our situation.

"Are we broke?" he questioned.

"Yup, I think so," I said.

"But for real this time?"

"This could be the Big One," I answered with conviction.

"Are you upset?"

I indulged in extreme understatement. "I was, you know, hoping we'd make it further."

He laughed. "I never thought we'd make it this far."

"Well. I'm warmed by your faith in us."

"Oh, sorry, should I pretend to have faith in you?"

"To my face," I joked. "You're only supposed to tell people your honest opinion when I'm not around."

"I'll remember that."

We drank a few rounds of beer while discussing the future of online publishing. At the time, people were wondering whether YouTube could survive, given it had no way to make money and was facing lawsuits because its users kept uploading pirated copyrighted material. Once we had proven to our satisfaction that YouTube was doomed, we stood up from the table to leave.

"Always be positive," he reminded me, tipping back his head and finishing off the last few drops of his stout.

"Pursue your passion," I reminded him.

He dramatically returned his glass to the table. "Believe in your dreams."

"Winners never quit and quitters never win."

"If you don't believe in yourself then who will?"

"The mind is the maker."

"A journey of a thousand miles begins with a single step," he declared.

"'No' is how you get to 'Yes'."

He pointed at me and gave me an order. "Be confident."

I pointed at him and did the same. "Be creative."

"Uh … um …" He paused to think. "Damn."

"Platitude shortage?"

"Seems like. You got anything?" He was dismayed at his own lack of quips.

I had one more. "How about this: today is the first day of the rest of your life."

"Not bad! And um …" he trailed off again. "You got anything else?"

"Nada."

"It's a sad day when two people in the tech industry can't think of vapid clichés to say to each other," he said.

"Wait a year and the industry will coin some more," I offered.

Later that week an investor gave us $100,000, and we were able to survive a bit longer.

47

Maybe John was now in that situation, needing to raise some money so Celolot could survive until he was given some other money that he'd already been promised. If only he demonstrated the slightest hint of humor, I think it would have made John more human to me. I believe it shows a lot of maturity to be able to face personal crisis with a sense of humor. Humility and self-awareness, too—these are qualities it would have been refreshing to see. But he seemed to be distorting the facts to fit whatever narrative he wanted us to believe, and re-writing that narrative on an almost daily basis. Either he was lying to us or he was lying to himself but, like most great salespeople, he lied very naturally. In my view, his own choices dehumanized him, and under the circumstances it was very difficult for me to feel any sympathy.

WEDNESDAY, JULY 15TH, 2015

I got to work at 11:00 A.M. John announced that our demo had stopped working. Sipping my coffee, I logged into the server to find out what the problem was. I looked at the error log for the API app, but it seemed okay. Then I checked the error log for the NLP app.

```
java.lang.StringIndexOutOfBoundsException: String index out of
range: -1
at java.lang.String.substring(String.java:1955)
at Celolot.nlp.Extractor.fuckBitchesGetMoney.java:87
```

What the hell was this?
"FuckBitchesGetMoney"?
What kind of name is that for a function?
A computer programmer can name their functions anything, but there are some "best practices" regarding names, and this particular function name violated all of them.
I asked Sital why he had given this name to his function. He looked at me straight, shrugged, and stated that the name was from the 1995 song by The Notorious B.I.G., "Get Money." I replied that rap lyrics were not part of our naming conventions. He promised that he would change it.
Coming from anyone else, I might have interpreted the function name

as an act of angry rebellion, but Sital was too forthright for that. Apparently, he thought the name was funny and went with it because he wanted to add some humor to his code. Never did he stop to think it might be unprofessional.

I looked through his code and found several other functions that had inappropriate names. I sent him a list and asked him to change their names to something standard.

A week later the function was still there. FuckBitchesGetMoney. Yet I don't think that any of this was a deliberate act of rebellion. He was just oddly forgetful and disorganized.

Friday, July 17th, 2015

In theory, it was payday. I had set up direct deposit, but no money appeared in my account. I emailed John about this. He wrote back to the whole team:

I totaly forgot to file paymnt with Paychex, sorr guys.

He'd been busy with other things. At first he said he'd push it through immediately, but then he ran into some trouble with the banks or the accountants, so he asked that we wait two more weeks and then get double the payment. A bit of a mess but we all rolled with it.

If I was with a crew that I trusted, then this incident would have been hilarious. But with this crew, it was worrisome.

Thankfully, we did eventually get paid.

Wednesday, July 22nd, 2015

Sital's code was getting better, but we knew it could break at any time—so I kept working on an app that would automatically test his code and alert us if Sital made any mistakes.

I emailed Hwan:

I asked John for a train ticket on Monday, but he said he needed more time to get a good price on tickets. He got me a ticket for August 3rd. So that is the next time I'll be down in DC

THURSDAY, JULY 23RD, 2015

The incubator tried very hard to exude the aura of a hip place where creative people could invent the future, so it offered fairly good coffee, as well as fairly good beer from a keg in the back of the office—all for free. However, no one had thought to set up a budget to buy milk or cream, so there was a jar near the coffee with a note on it saying that we had to put in fifty cents any time we used the milk. The bottom of the note read, "If we don't get enough money to pay for the milk, we will no longer be able to provide milk." So the beer was free but the milk was expensive.

These kinds of minor inconsistencies tend to spring up in any large organization, and since the incubator was part of NYU and subsidized by the government of New York, for all I knew getting free milk might have required a vote by the state legislature. I was happy to pay, though of course the whole situation was comical.

MONDAY, JULY 27TH, 2015

We were making progress. Late in the day I video conferenced with Hwan and Sital.

We still needed a way for Sital's app to pose follow-up questions to the users of the iPhone app. Hwan made clear that some additional design work needed to be done before he could add the feedback questions to the iPhone app.

Sital and I would combine efforts to pull contact and product names from Salesforce. Whenever a salesperson mentioned someone, like "Carol," we needed to be able to find out who that Carol was. If she was listed in the salesperson's contacts, then we should be able deduce her full name without the salesperson having to write, "Carol Harrington who works at Sheraton Hotels."

We agreed that within two weeks John would be able to do demos using the iPhone app.

I live up on Ninety-Eighth Street. I decided to walk home along the Hudson River. There were people walking their dogs, sitting on the grass, and having a picnic with friends. Some were smoking cigarettes, some were smoking weed, some were drinking wine. As the sun neared the horizon, the atmosphere stripped away all the shorter electro-magnetic frequencies—blue, indigo, violet—and the remaining long frequencies, like red, interacted with the few wisps of clouds to give the sense of curtains closing on a grand theater. I admired our 4.5 billion-year-old nuclear explosion, 150 million kilometers away, from which we derive all energy. The light, still reflecting off the top of the atmosphere, also reflected off the river and the wake of each boat.

The grandeur of this daily natural event has a way of putting things in perspective. Despite all the problems with the project, we were creating something useful and possibly important. In truth, we had made huge progress in two and a half months. In two more weeks we would put an actual product in people's hands, and we would start to see what their real reactions were.

TUESDAY, JULY 28TH, 2015

And then, everything changed.

When I arrived at work, I found John irate and somewhat confused. He told me we were giving up on the iPhone app, and we would fire Hwan.

"But keep that a secret!" he urged. "I don't want to tell Hwan."

It was as if I'd been driving through intense fog with only a vague idea of how poor my visibility had been, and now I had hit something that confirmed how blind I was. I tried my best to remain composed.

"You don't want to tell Hwan that you're about to fire him?"

"Not yet. Just keep it a secret."

This was the beginning of what I would later call our Big Pivot—we were suddenly giving up on most of the work we had done over the summer and going in a different direction. Pivoting is actually a pretty common occurrence at startups. Eric Ries, in his book *The Lean Startup*, defines a pivot as "a structured course correction designed to test a new fundamental hypothesis about the product, strategy, and engine of growth."

But in our case, the question was, *Why?* Why were we giving up on our iPhone app? John said he had talked to Milburn, and the two of them agreed that the iPhone app was too complex. It had too many screens. It had too many buttons. It was everything that salespeople hated. Getting away from that kind of complexity was exactly why Celolot had been created. Simplicity in all things: that had to be our motto.

Instead of our custom app, we would use the standard messaging app that comes with every iPhone. The average salesperson sent text messages all day, every day, and now Celolot would be just another number in their phonebook. John was very excited about this—the salespeople already had all the software they needed to connect to us! Nobody wants to learn more software, and Celolot would have faced an uphill battle trying to get anyone to install their app! John insisted he would have never been able to sell the software that Hwan was building.

It seemed that the leadership had lost confidence in the product almost overnight. After months of pleasant daydreams about all the money they would soon be making, the euphoria had suddenly ended.

Whenever you deal with hysteria, the most important thing to do is confront it directly. So I attempted to fight the fear with reason.

"Why are we doing this now?" I inquired. "We're almost done with our product."

"We need to go faster!" He was waving his hands for emphasis. His gesticulations suggested, "This is a crisis and you just don't get it!"

"Okay, remember, all startups contain an element of risk. The important thing is to manage that risk as wisely as possible."

"We've been wise all summer!" His tone communicated frustration with my incomprehension. "We've been way too wise! Our product is going to burn up all of our money!"

I did a quick calculation in my head. My original assumption had been that we were all being paid the same amount, and that if you added up the salary and the benefits and the taxes, that worked out to something like $150,000 or $160,000 a year for each of us. That implied $12,500 a month, so for the four of us, $50,000 a month. Web servers and other incidentals, like my train tickets, might be another $10,000, and that was a high estimate. John had indicated that Sital was actually being paid less than us. We'd been working less than three full months. So at the high end of any reasonable estimate, $60,000 a month, we had at most gone through $180,000. At this rate, we would burn through $720,000 during the first year, leaving us with $580,000 for the second year. So what was the trigger for the current nightmare delirium? Either they never had $1.3 million, or they had some wild, surreptitious expenses. They had hired that design firm in Brooklyn, but how much could they have possibly wasted there? $50,000?

"I thought we had over a million," I said. "Surely we've only touched a fraction of that?"

"Yeah, but, we've got to build a business! A real business! Where do we get the money for that? We need to hire a bunch of salesmen! Without a sales team, we are dead. Don't you see? This whole process has been dragging on for way too long!"

"Well, I agree, but you and I both know the reason for those delays. So let's do something about Sital!"

"Sital is not the one who's been slowing us down!" he shouted.

"Sital is not the one who's been slowing us down?" I was astounded. "Then *who* has been slowing us down?"

"*Hwan's* been taking too long!"

"Hwan's been taking too long!" Now I was outraged. "Hwan has been busy because you hired a design firm in Brooklyn that created an interface consisting entirely of custom widgets! We ended up with eye candy instead of utility! And you loved those designs! If we had simply used the standard design elements that Apple makes available to every developer, then Hwan would have been done a month ago!"

"Well, now is not the time to try to pin the blame on anyone." He was peevish.

"Oh, so, now is not the time to pin the blame on anyone, but we're going to fire Hwan?" I asked.

"No, no, no ... not necessarily fire him. I just think, uh, I just think that we, um ... We need to rethink his role at the company."

"What will his new role at the company be?"

"Well, we need to think about that." He retreated like a coward. "Hey, listen, don't talk about any of this with Hwan, okay? This has to be a secret."

"Wonderful!" I shouted. I didn't feel wonderful.

I promptly walked to my desk and wrote Hwan a long message on Slack, giving him a heads-up that the company was switching focus away from his app. I did not say that the company was thinking of firing him, but I knew he was smart enough to understand the implication. I was going to DC on Monday, so we would soon have a face-to-face conversation about what was happening.

Then John came up to me and told me that we had to use Twilio to connect the iPhone to our servers. I asked why we were using Twilio. He just repeated that we had to use Twilio; the decision had already been made.

I was irritated by this declaration, which seemed to come completely out of nowhere. John tasked me with researching how the connection would be done, and since I didn't know much about Twilio, I spent the rest of the day reading about it.

Twilio is extremely cool, and in a different scenario I would be excited to use it. Using Twilio meant that we would have a phone number that people could use to send messages to our servers. Instead of installing new software, people could simply send us text messages. And we wouldn't need Hwan anymore.

But Twilio would be a very dangerous step for us. If John and the Celo-lot Board of Directors really wanted us to ditch our iPhone app, this meant that we would be 100% committing ourselves to English as our only inter-face—and building a flawless NLP engine would be indispensable. There would be no buttons, no forms, nothing to click on. Just words and phrases written in English, submitted by innumerable users. If we failed to build an NLP engine that could understand all of it, then we were doomed. I thought NLP was a fantastic supplement to traditional interfaces, but as a complete replacement, it was a huge gamble. It was like jumping out of an airplane without a spare parachute. Furthermore, if we had Hwan build us an app, then we could customize it in some really cool ways. Special messages, special ways of allowing data to be edited—things that are not possible with the standard iPhone Message app.

As I walked home that night, I thought about this new direction. I had three conflicting thoughts:

First: This was awesome! We were going to try to build a pure NLP experience for our users. Neither Google nor Facebook—nor even Ap-ple—had tried this yet. Any time an entrepreneur wanted to pay me good money to work on something insanely ambitious, my response was, "Sign me up!" This was my idea of fun.

Second: Whoa! Neither Google nor Facebook—nor even Apple—had tried this yet! And we were the team that was going to make this work? With *Sital* as our NLP expert?

Third: Wait, we were doing this because we needed to go faster? How did that make sense? We'd been working on a somewhat traditional prod-uct with somewhat known parameters. From this point forward, we would be a pure research project. This made sense if we were trying to win an award for innovation, but it made absolutely no sense if we were trying to go faster.

Wednesday, July 29th, 2015

We spent the entire day in a conference room talking about Twilio. At one point we had a phone call with a Twilio representative. Unfortunately, we did not fit into their standard customer profile. The representative had to find a specialist who could talk to us about our unique case. We waited an hour, and then we had another conversation with someone from Twilio.

After we got off the conference call, we all sat there for a moment without saying anything, as if we had shocked ourselves with the knowledge of what we were about to undertake. There were many nuances to using Twilio, and we were only now starting to consider them, whereas the nuances of using Hwan's app had been carefully considered all summer.

"What does our CTO think of this?" I asked.

John looked confused. He blinked. "Who?"

"Dennis." I stated this simply at first, since I couldn't imagine why I needed to remind him who Dennis was. When he said nothing, I continued: "Our CTO. What does he think of this?"

"Oh," he said. He looked puzzled. "Um, I don't think he has an opinion on it."

"Have you talked to him about it?"

"I don't think he has an opinion," he repeated.

"Let me see if I get this straight." I ran my hand over my face and took a deep breath. "Our board of directors has a very strong opinion about whether we should use Twilio, but our CTO does not have any opinion at all?"

"Let's not bother Dennis right now. Let's stay focused on getting our work done."

I had the impression that Dennis was gone and he was not coming back. Perhaps John already knew this but didn't want to tell us.

Thursday, July 30th, 2015

We were supposed to meet to discuss our Twilio strategy. Sital forgot about the meeting and was working from home. We sent him several reminders on Slack, and when he finally saw them, he responded with half a line.

Sital
aw crap I totally for got

He arrived an hour later, at which point we started the meeting.

Hwan was not asked to participate in this meeting. In fact, he was not even told about it. I asked that we reach out to him and have him join us via video, but John refused. I got the impression that he was scared to confront Hwan.

At lunchtime, I went for a two-hour walk and tried to think through the exact mechanics of how we would handle conversations with humans. I did not want to work another twenty-three-hour shift, like the one before the canceled demo. I did not want us up against another deadline, ambushed by things we had not considered. I wanted to get all of the difficult "edge cases" written down so that when we inevitably had to deal with them, I would have it in writing that John had known about them up front.

I decided that tomorrow I would confront John with the real complexity of what we were about to do.

FRIDAY, JULY 31ST, 2015

I went to check out Sital's code, and I saw that, once again, he had gone a week without committing any code to GitHub. I wrote to him and reminded him to commit his work every day. I felt like a professor reminding him to get his term paper in before the deadline.

John and I had another long meeting to discuss Twilio. Among the leadership, the old euphoria regarding the iPhone app had been replaced by the new euphoria regarding Twilio. Apparently, Twilio was so good that it spared us the need to do any hard thinking. I felt the new euphoria was even more misplaced than the old euphoria, so I set out to challenge it.

"Imagine a salesperson wants to edit an old Opportunity. Do they write 'I want to edit an old Opportunity'? That's a lot of writing compared to simply clicking a button."

John furrowed his brow, thought about this for a second, and then offered, "They can just type 'edit Opportunity'."

"Okay, good. And what should we do if they write something ambiguous, like 'Opportunity'?"

"We should assume they want to create a new Opportunity."

"Okay, good." This dialogue was going exactly the way I had anticipated. "And what should we do if they write something else ambiguous, like 'edit'?"

"We ask them a follow-up question, such as 'What would you like to edit?'"

"Okay, good. And where do we store the current state of the conversation?"

"What do you mean?"

"There has to be a place in our software where we keep track of the fact that we just asked them a question," I explained. "Otherwise we won't know how to deal with the response."

"Why?"

"Well for instance, what if they send us just 'edit'?"

"I just told you! We ask them a follow-up question, like 'What would you like to edit?'"

"What if the response is 'Opportunity'?"

"That's so obvious! If the response is 'Opportunity,' then they want to edit an Opportunity. Why are you trying to make this complicated?"

"You just said that 'Opportunity' should imply that they want to create a new Opportunity, not edit an old one."

"Oh." He appeared momentarily stumped. We sat in silence for a moment while he thought about it.

"We can no longer respond in a simple way to what they send us," I explained. "We are now engaging in conversations, and we need to track the state of the conversation. If they only send us one word, we need to be able to read that one word in context. And teaching context to a computer is a very complicated undertaking."

"Um ... uh ... okay, tell you what. From now on, we will just default to assuming that 'Opportunity' means 'edit an old Opportunity'."

"Okay, good. And how will they create new Opportunities?"

"Um, then they have to write 'new Opportunity.'"

"Okay, good. And what happens if they only write 'new'?"

"Uh, I told you, we ask them a follow-up question. We ask them what they would like to create."

"Okay, good. And what if the answer is 'Opportunity'?"

John paused for about four long seconds before speaking. "Oh shit."

"Look, John, there's no way to make this simple. When we simplify the interface for the user, we increase the complexity of what the computer programmers have to do."

I was pretty sure he wasn't listening to me. In his head, he was repeating the conversation we'd just had, trying to see if he could spot a flaw in my reasoning.

"Giving up on a traditional interface is bold, but dangerous," I continued. "There might be moments when we want to take a hybrid approach. So it might be useful to have Hwan on the team."

"Uh, let me think about this," he waffled. He seemed unsettled that there was an angle which he couldn't dismiss.

Our meeting ended. He left. I am not sure where he went. Maybe he was meeting potential customers, or investors, or maybe he was going to talk to Milburn again.

I met with Sital and I repeated the conversation that I'd just had with John. I was trying to get both them to realize the complexity of what we were about to do. Without a traditional interface for users to interact with, we were going to have to build software that could handle entire conversations with humans.

What would our options be if we had a message app of our own—something that looked just like the Message app that Apple includes on every iPhone, but something we could control and customize as we needed?

I reached out to Hwan on Slack.

lkrubncr
Hwan, I am curious, given our shifting priorities, how long would it take you to develop a message app? I mean, suppose that you stop all work on the current app?

Hwan
Are we really stopping? Are we giving up on the current app?

lkrubner
Let's assume that we are. Suppose we completely abandon the current app and you can devote 100% of your time to a new app. How long would that take you?

Hwan
I suppose 4 to 6 weeks

lkrubner
Is that the fastest you can do it?

Hwan
Well, what does it need to look like?

Ikrubner

Eventually, it should look just like the Apple Message app, but for now, I mean, what is the absolute most basic thing you can get working?

Hwan

Maybe something in 3 to 4 weeks. But it will be ugly.

Ikrubner

Ugly is okay for now. We just need to be quick.

Hwan

Is the company out of money?

Ikrubner

I doubt it, but I'm really not sure. John is feeling pressure, but I don't know exactly why.

Hwan

Okay. I'll see you Monday?

Ikrubner

Yes, I'll see you on Monday.

Hwan

They have the money to buy you a ticket?

Ikrubner

That or I'll buy it myself.

MONDAY, AUGUST 3RD, 2015

I woke up at 4:30 A.M. to catch the 6:00 A.M. train so I could meet Hwan at our office in DC by 10:00 A.M.

Were we really going to fire him? More than most days, Hwan and I spent time talking about the company rather than about our technology.

It hardly made sense to talk seriously about our software when everything might be thrown away in a week.

Confrontation was essential, because honesty was essential. I demanded that we have a team video meeting, with Hwan and I on one side and John and Sital on the other. When John hesitated, I argued that an early-stage startup needed to be a transparent learning organization, or it ends up dead.

Everyone was polite. John complimented the team on how hard everyone had been working and how much creativity everyone had shown. Responding to the theme of creativity, Hwan outlined some of the cool things we could do if we controlled a messaging app of our own. In particular, we could have custom fields that allowed the editing of specific values. Not only was this a good idea, it reminded me why I felt that we had to keep Hwan on staff. We were getting zero ideas from our so-called NLP expert. Hwan grasped the real potential of what mobile technologies offered the world.

I left WeWork at 8:00 P.M. and took Amtrak back to New York. I arrived at my apartment well past midnight. My days in DC were long, but I felt that we only had sane team dynamics when Hwan was included as a true equal.

Tuesday, August 4th, 2015

I studied the academic literature regarding computers simulating conversations. What we were about to attempt was very much on the edge of the new.

(Unknown to us, Amazon and Google were both racing to offer voice interfaces for conversations, and these would begin to appear in late 2015 and 2016. This is part of the experience of being in a startup doing something cutting-edge: the market you target appears wide open, as if you were the first person on Earth to have thought about building your idea, but it always turns out that hundreds of other startups had discovered the same idea, at roughly the same time, and are racing toward the same market.)

Up until now, the best the tech industry had managed to offer as a way of tracking conversations was Apple's "Siri" personality, but for the most part Siri only handled one question-and-answer interaction at a time. For instance, if you ask, "Siri, what is the temperature?" then Siri says something like, "It is eighty-nine degrees outside." If you say, "Siri, wake me up at 6:00 A.M.," then Siri says, "Your alarm is set for 6:00 A.M." That is simple. But tracking entire conversations meant tracking the accumulated meaning of dozens of interactions.

The crucial point is that we needed to have an app that focused on tracking the current state of each conversation that we were having with each user. The technical jargon for this kind of software is Finite State Machine (FSM).

FRIDAY, AUGUST 7TH, 2015

Our collective hunger for resolution forced a moment of true candor. We met in a conference room and Hwan joined us by video.

John had talked it over with the board, and they all agreed that the company would be stronger if we built our own Message app rather than rely on Twilio.

So Hwan was back to work, building a completely new app.

John admitted that he had made a mistake by trying to hide so much from us. He specifically thanked Hwan for his input. Then he said that an early-stage startup needed to be a transparent learning organization (I was pleased that he used one of my phrases) and that from now on we should be 100% honest with each other about whatever we were learning.

I felt great hope about our ability to move forward, but it was ephemeral. This would be the only occasion when I felt that John was being entirely forthright with us.

Unfortunately, we had lost more than a week because of the board's insistence on Twilio—and worse, we had so utterly exhausted ourselves fighting over it that we never got around to the subject of the Big Pivot itself. And there was a great deal that we should have discussed, as a company, regarding the Big Pivot.

Friday, August 14th, 2015

Sital spent the week attempting to write the code that could function as our Conversation FSM. However, he could not write anything that worked. There were many frameworks and libraries of software whose purpose was to help computer programmers create FSMs, but as before, he found all libraries confusing. He felt certain that, given enough time, he could figure out how to write an FSM. I'm sure that is true, but "given enough time" might mean "two or three years." We needed him to come up with something in a week or two. For the sake of moving quickly, the appropriate strategy would involve the use of a library of code that specialized in the task of creating FSMs. I made this suggestion multiple times, to Sital and John. At the start of the week, John suggested we give Sital more time. By the end of the week, John seemed as frustrated as I was.

Wednesday, August 19th, 2015

John was freaked out. We needed to make progress, but Sital was about to go on a ten-day vacation. John gave us all a long speech about the need to make money. Sital promised to have his code working before he left, but I was doubtful.

Friday, August 21st, 2015

Sital was at the airport, flying to Hawaii. I tried to use his software but it died with an error. I wrote to him, he made some quick edits, I tried again, and it still died. Then he was off on vacation, and I was left to deal with his terrible code.

That evening John and I checked in on Slack.

John
Can you get stuff don this week?

lkrubner
I can focus on Salesforce for a week. Or I could try to rewrite the NLP code. The only question is, what is the #1 priority?

John
I hate to say iit, but possibly te NLP issues, because wwe dont have time for thiis shiit anmore

lkrubner
Okay, let me look at his code.

Later, John sent me an email:

Ar yo abll too work on this without Sital?

I responded:

For sure, but I wish things werc differenl. His code is an incredible mess. He is unable to handle 2 big parts that his app needs to handle:
   1.) figuring out the current state of the conversation
   2.) handling more than 1 conversation at a time (concurrency)

Then John sent me the following, via email, later that night:

I totally understand your frustration. His abilities, and especially his lack of abilities, have become completely transparent. He is a brilliantly creative data scientist of incredible genius, but he lacks certain engineering skills that we need. Unfortunately, in the future, we will need just such a data scientist as him. He won't like it, but we may have to limit his role to Chief Data Scientist and nothing more.
   I'm thinking of two options for moving forward while he's gone.
   1) I'll bring in someone to work on the concurrency issues, so you can mostly focus on the Salesforce integration.
   2) You can go through his code and clean it up while he's gone, then you can go back to the Salesforce integration.
   I'll let you decide based on whatever you think would be most efficient for us.

Again, I understand your frustrations, as I feel them too. The situation has evolved in a manner to no one's liking. However, we're not going to make any rash decisions, nor any core changes to the team, however gratifying that might be. We will need him to train data and maintain NLP engines for our customers (when we have customers).

Per his habits, I've had multiple conversations with him. And when he gets back I will make clear to him that we're done with second chances: if you don't act like a responsible adult, then you don't get treated with the freedoms of one. So from now he will face these rules:

* • *No more YouTube for him in the office.*
* • *He will be in the office everyday no later than 10am.*
* • *He will be required to push his code to GitHub everyday at noon and 5pm.*

Take care,
John

What the hell? Here was an immaculate, professionally written letter, without any spelling errors. The grammar was perfect, words were capitalized, and sentences ended in periods. It was unlike anything that John had previously written to me—and something about it was off. Why would John describe Sital as "a brilliantly creative data scientist of incredible genius"? I couldn't believe that John thought those words were true.

And what did he mean when he wrote, "we may have to limit his role to Chief Data Scientist and nothing more"? What else could his role *be*? Sital would never become ... my mind went blank. The CTO? John was admitting that Sital would never become the CTO? As if anyone had ever considered that?

What sort of lunacy was this?

SUNDAY, AUGUST 30TH, 2015

Sital was still away on vacation, so I mostly worked from home. I wrote to John on Slack.

lkrubner
Multi-threading the NLP app has been easy, but the real test happens when we can test real conversations with it. The way Sital

wrote the conversation code is very rigid.

John
Totlly understood. Whatwe thinkmng timeline wise on hhen the hard part will be goood to go?

lkrubner
I look forward to testing everything tomorrow. I believe we can have a kind of NLP conversation. But there are deep problems in the way Sital tracks the state of each conversation. I have been writing him private notes on Slack, with feedback about mistakes he made. I think we can create the illusion of something working by the 10th, but after that I would like to substantially re-write the code.

He had an odd response to my use of the word "illusion."

John
Illusion to where s working and usable? Would a like a enjoy customer using it?

In retrospect, I regret the answer that I gave:

lkrubner
It will work. The conversation will need a lot of fine-tuning. That will take months. But we can have something that basically works on the 10th.

Failing to clarify that I meant only an illusion would work—not a true app that we could ask money for—was my worst misstep. I would spend the next several weeks trying to pull back the expectations set by this clumsily-worded email.

Of course, it says something about how strongly John wanted to avoid bad news, and how desperate he was for good news, that he latched on to this one email and ignored the next several that I was to send.

The board of directors would be meeting on September 17. We would be ready to offer them a demo, but not a real working product.

Monday, August 31st, 2015

I had spent the past month studying the academic and informal literature on FSMs. We were truly on the cutting edge; most of the best articles were less than twelve months old, written by other companies working on the same issue. As I studied the subject, I gained a more accurate idea about how difficult our task was. A good programmer, working long hours, could get it done in four weeks. If, for some reason, we got a computer programmer who could only work part time, then the Conversation FSM would take closer to eight weeks.

I put all this into an email. My estimate would prove to be highly accurate and highly unwelcome. I reminded John that on the twenty-first he had written, "I'll bring in someone to work on the concurrency issues, so you can mostly focus on the Salesforce integration." I added:

> I have a small project for someone. Would it be possible to bring in another programmer for 4 weeks? We need a small app that can manage our conversations as Finite State Machines. The FSM code would know which stage and branch our conversations are at. This would be a small app, but an important one. It needs to be done right.

He didn't respond.

Tuesday, September 1st, 2015

I got to the office early, but apparently John was out all day at meetings. I hadn't heard from him, so I wrote him another email:

> If I am to focus on the Salesforce integration, then we need to bring in someone who can create our Conversation FSM. This will be the most important software at Celolot. Everything else is just a sideshow. Since we have decided to have a purely conversational interface, the Conversation FSM is the core of what we are building.

John wrote back to say we were over-budget for outside consultants, and we needed to cut back.

I asked him what had changed in the last ten days. Back on August 21st, he had been the one who suggested we bring in an outsider.

He asked if this was really necessary. I tried to clarify for him that the choice was between spending money versus progressing more slowly. I could write the Conversation FSM myself, but it would take me a month. After that I could work on the Salesforce integration. If we went down that road, then we would not be ready until November. Was that what he wanted? Or did he want to hire someone new, who could take this task off of my hands?

I refrained from repeating my point that this work would normally be handled by our NLP expert, but we were working with a beginner, so we lacked that option.

John wrote back and suggested that for our first iteration we leave out the Conversation FSM. I wrote back and explained that that would not be possible—when the board of directors had committed us to the Big Pivot, they had also committed us to building a Conversation FSM. What I'd come to realize was that this was the core meaning of the Big Pivot: becoming a company that could track the state of the current conversation. John wrote back and said the pivot had nothing to do with FSM, no one had agreed to that. I wrote back and tried to explain that the board of directors had committed us to the FSM, whether they knew it or not.

In his view, we didn't have the money to build this. He again suggested that there had to be some way to leave out the Conversation FSM. I insisted it was impossible to proceed without an FSM, at which point he once again asserted that Sital was our NLP expert and therefore would take care of it.

I was filled with a toxic mix of disgust and rage. Yet again I was witnessing bizarre leadership antics derail a fantastic project. Given the ambitious nature of the technology our reliance on Sital was clearly idiotic.

For now, I was willing to rededicate myself to the surprisingly difficult task of making John see the obstacles in front of us. He would need to learn fast. I was only willing to push a rock uphill for another month or so. If we got to mid-October and he still seemed oblivious, my anger would transform into cynical detachment, and I would begin to look for another job.

I reminded him of the discussion that he and I had had on July 31, about the difficulty of figuring out what a salesperson meant when they wrote the word "Opportunity." If he'd understood that on the thirty-first then why didn't he understand that now?

Finally, John caved. If I wrote up a formal job description for the project, he said, he would find someone. I typed up the basics of what we needed and sent it over.

Thursday, September 3rd, 2015

When I read over the contract announcement that John had posted to the freelancer sites, I was somewhere between confused and annoyed.

I wrote to John:

I notice you put a price of $5,000 on this project. How did you arrive at that number? If a freelancer charges $60 an hour, which is cheap, then 4 weeks of work would be $9,600. I doubt we can get anyone who is qualified who will do this for as little as $5,000.

He was at various meetings all over the city, so he never came to the office. I didn't hear from him during the day.

In the evening, I sent him another email, in which I tried to convey how critical the Conversation FSM was. If we were going to track whole conversations, then the code that tracked those conversations was the core objective of the company. I wrote:

I want to emphasize that this will be the most important software at Celolot. Everything else is just a sideshow. Everything will depend on our Conversation code. Without it, we are nothing.

I never got a response to that. Was I using the wrong words? Or was he so terrified that he couldn't hear me? Perhaps John and Milburn were in denial regarding the ambition of what they had committed themselves to.

In a sense, what we were doing was idiotic. Anyone who viewed our situation objectively would say that Celolot needed three highly-skilled, full-time programmers. Yet now we were bringing in someone, hopefully someone good, but limiting them to part time—just so we could keep another programmer, who we knew to be unskilled, on a full-time salary. Was all this just to avoid the emotional trauma of firing someone?

We would move into the autumn with two good programmers working full time, a novice programmer working full time, and another good programmer working part time. This was definitely not my preference, but it was the best compromise that I could wrest from John.

Friday, September 4th, 2015

We had gotten some responses to the job posting, so I spent the day conducting interviews.

I talked to a half-dozen people who were simply not experienced enough to do what we needed. We hardly needed another Sital on staff.

I spoke with a brilliant guy who had done interesting work modeling physics and building computer simulations. There were several videos of him on YouTube at various workshops he had taught, and I watched them and asked him follow-up questions. He seemed hyper-intelligent, but also very eccentric.

Next, I did a Skype interview with a guy named Gregory. When he came up on the screen, he seemed to be in a college dorm room, though he looked like he was in his mid-twenties or even older. He was sitting in a bunk next to a huge, pink, furry toy panda. Behind him was a pennant for George Mason University. Possibly a graduate student. We introduced ourselves and made small talk. After a few minutes I decided to make a joke about it.

"What's with the pink panda?"

"What? Oh, that's my girlfriend's. Yeah, I'm in my girlfriend's dorm room. Yeah, if you're wondering about all the pink, this is a girl's dorm room. I live in Pittsburgh. I'm just down in DC visiting her."

"Ah, I see."

Gregory was not quite as experienced as the first guy I had talked to, but he had done some tremendous projects, and he showed a great deal of energy. We had not yet decided whom to hire. Showing an admirable willingness to take the initiative, he took it on himself to search Clojure libraries for FSMs and even put together a little demo of how he would approach the subject.

Saturday, September 5th, 2015

John wrote to me to ask how the various job interviews had gone.

explained that I'd talked to two people who were good: an eccentric genius, and another guy who seemed very competent and hardworking. I suggested that John talk to both of them to figure out if he had a preference.

Then John wrote: *And, just for my edification, we'll be ready to use the whole platform on Tuesday?*

There are certain patterns that we only see in retrospect. Months later, when I finally reread all of the email from my time at Celolot, I noticed that this message again had no spelling errors, and the word "edification" did not sound like a word that John would use. I now suspect that, as we got into the autumn, more and more of the messages which supposedly came from John were really being written by someone else.

All I could say in response was that we were working hard and doing our best. He reminded me that the board of directors would meet on the seventeenth and they expected to see a working product.

MONDAY, SEPTEMBER 7TH, 2015

John and I were at the office. Suddenly, I recalled that we had been told that the "founders" had gone away for ninety-day summer internships at Microsoft and Google and were supposed to come back in September.

I turned to John and asked him, "Hey, when is Dennis coming back?"

"Dennis?" John seemed surprised by the question. Then he furrowed his brow. "Why?"

"You said he was coming back in the autumn."

"Oh." He paused and thought about that a moment. "Uh, he's got other plans."

"He's not coming back?"

"Um ... uh ... um ... not really."

"That's a pretty big deal, isn't it?" I asked.

"Uh, why?" He sounded extremely wary of whatever I might say next.

"We've lost our CTO."

"Oh!" This seemed to be the first time the idea had occurred to him. "Yeah, well, don't worry about it."

"Does the board of directors know that we've lost our CTO?"

"Yeah, they know. Don't worry about it."

70

I wanted to make sure I understood correctly. "So we've lost our CTO, but the board is not concerned. Is that what you're telling me?"

"It's all good. Everything is good. Don't worry about it."

"Are you angry at Dennis?" I asked.

"What?" His head snapped up. "Why would I be angry at Dennis?"

"For abandoning you."

He seemed to think the question was bizarre. "No! Uh, no, it's all good. Everything is good. Dennis is good. I'm good. Seriously man, everyone is good. Don't worry about it."

The whole thing felt like a ruse, as if they'd always known that Dennis was not coming back. I was tempted to ask if we would hire a new CTO, or even offer to take on the role myself, just to see how deep the lies went. Lying seemed to be bred into the DNA of this startup.

Even three months later, in December, when I checked the listing for Celolot in an online database, Dennis was still listed as the CTO. Very odd.

Tuesday, September 8th, 2015

I had partly rescued the bad code that Sital had written in August, and now I gave it back to him, hoping he could finish it. He promptly broke it again. We soon realized that we had a lot of work still to do getting the apps to talk to each other, and we could not rely on Sital for anything. Hwan was worried about the situation and asked for a telephone conference so that he and I could discuss it openly with John.

Hwan and I both now made the case, as strongly as possible, that Sital was a danger to the company. United, we stated that we would lose faith in the future of the company if John continued to support Sital. I recounted the numerous incidents that had occurred over the last four months that gave us reason to fire Sital. Hwan expressed the fear that Celolot was running out of money, or would run out of money if we had nothing to sell. John jumped in and reassured him: Celolot had plenty of money and we should not worry about the financial condition of the company. Additionally, he said that they were about to close another round of funding, so they'd be all set for a year.

"You can never be sure about funding," I countered.

"We can be sure," said John. "Trust me. We have this money. It's already locked in."

I didn't pursue that angle. I pointed out that we had missed every deadline so far because of delays that traced back to Sital, and we would continue to miss deadlines so long as we depended on him.

"Okay," John finally agreed. "You guys are right. He's dragging us down. We gave him plenty of second chances, but he hasn't improved. He's bad for the company."

"So we'll fire him?" I asked.

"Yes, for sure," John assured us. "How about we fire him in three weeks?"

"Why three weeks?" I asked.

"We just need to close this current round of funding, and then we will fire him. And we'll have the money to get someone really good."

"But you can't be sure about the money," I repeated.

"In this case, we can be sure about the money." He seemed entirely confident on this subject.

"If that's true, then that's a reasonable plan," I agreed. "We fire him in three weeks, and hire someone better."

"That is good news!" said Hwan.

"Yeah, it's my fault," said John. "I let this drag on for too long. I should have acted sooner."

"What's important is what we do next!" Hwan urged us to stay focused on our goals.

"Yes," I said. "Can we get someone as good as Arthur?"

"Maybe we can get Arthur," said John. "We will have the money, once this next round closes. I'll reach out to him."

"We might bring in Arthur full time?" I was astounded again, but finally in a good way. "That would be truly fantastic!"

"Yes," John affirmed. "I'll talk to him. As soon as this next round closes, we'll move to build a quality team."

Hwan was professional but was sure to give John an indication of how happy he was about the decision. "This really changes my perception of where we're going."

"Well, it's my fault," John repeated. "I should've acted sooner."

We all congratulated each other on the new direction of the company, and then we hung up.

And for a few days, I actually felt something that resembled hope regarding the future of the company.

Thursday, September 10th, 2015

Two days later, John dropped a bombshell: Sital must interview Gregory and approve of hiring him. Flabbergasted, I shared the diktat with Hwan. At first he assumed I was joking, but I insisted that I was repeating what John had said to me.

Later that day, Hwan and I got on a conference call with John. We had all agreed that Sital was a terrible programmer, so much that we wanted to fire him—but now we were going to trust his judgment about whom we should hire next? This struck me and Hwan as ludicrous. John felt like this was common sense: only an NLP expert could evaluate an NLP expert. I argued that Sital was not an NLP expert. John insisted that Sital needed to talk to Gregory.

I recounted every delay from the summer. John agreed that Sital had been problematic, but if he was going to leave, then he would have to leave on good terms. I was unclear what was being implied. John suggested that others respected Sital. I asked who that would be, but he didn't answer me. I asked John if he would be happy when Sital was gone. He said yes, he'd be very relieved when Sital was gone.

Later that night, out of sheer frustration, I wrote to John and asked him to again deliberate over this idea of Sital interviewing Gregory. John wrote back with a repeat of what he'd written on August 21:

He is a brilliantly creative data scientist of incredible genius.

This would become par for the course. When I spoke to John face to face, he'd verbally admit that Sital had been the source of immense problems—but whenever John communicated in written form (i.e., anything that could be later shown in a court of law), Sital remained "a brilliantly creative data scientist of incredible genius."

Friday, September 11th, 2015

At noon, Sital interviewed Gregory. If Sital had any suspicions that we wanted him fired, and if he wanted to safeguard his own job, he certainly had an opportunity. Someone with a math background could easily think of a trick question that would make Gregory look bad, but here we were rescued by Sital's childlike honesty. His conclusions were in line with my own: that Gregory was not an NLP specialist, but he was very smart, he studied hard, and he was competent in a lot of different areas.

When I left work later on, and stepped out into the warm evening air, I could see the new World Trade Center gleaming in the distance, taller than any other structure in the city. The sight triggered a meditation on resilience as I walked home. Greatness isn't achievable without resilience. Hopefully Celolot possessed this quality.

Monday, September 14th, 2015

John wrote to me on Slack. I found this angle really aggravating.

John
Just spoke to Gregory. He loves startups and lves what we do and do environment. He is very intrested in the fll-ttime. He has another good job ofer but it's a corporate environment, so he would like do t contract work F S&M app (mayb good understanding of the NLP/NLP app. Then afteweek or two, hel evaluate how he likes working with us, and we'll get a good understanding of we like working with him. a good understanding of o we like working Then after 2 weeks if we like hiim and he. likes us helltart fultime ledingg development of NLP and FSM app, OR if we stil like him and he decides to go t other job, he said since its corporate 8-430, hed still want to do contract work if we'd like. Sobest both worlds, we get see him before commmiting and he too he does.

There was still no agreement to hire Gregory! I tried to address this.

lkrubner
When is Gregory starting?

John
notsure. I need talk to Board

lkrubner
Do you realize this will delay the whole project?

John
no, no n delay

lkrubner
We won't have a fully working product until we have a working FSM app.

John
no, just finish NLP and API

lkrubner
The NLP won't work without the FSM.

John
Yes, it will. I aasked Sital. He says itll work

lkrubner
The system won't work. You and I had this conversation in July.

John
no delays. Sital sys it works

lkrubner
Given a sentence, I'm sure the NLP app can find fields such as Product and Amount, but we won't know what response to send to the user. Remember? We talked about this.

John
k, i will talk to Milburn

lkrubner
Why?

John
need Bord approval

lkrubner
You understand that we will run late if we don't get someone working on the FSM app?

John
I will talk to board, but move forwardd in the eantime

None of this communicated the absolute urgency of the Conversation
FSM, so I asked to meet John in person. I was at the incubator but he was
presently out meeting people. (Potential investors? Potential customers? I
didn't know.)

That evening John came to the office. We found a conference room
where we could speak privately. I emphasized how central the Conversation FSM was to everything we wanted to do. He nodded his head at
everything I said. He seemed to understand. Yet a few days later, it would
be as if we never spoke.

I admit, asking an outsider like Gregory to work on the Conversation FSM was most controversial idea that I pushed while at Celolot.
Months later, a lot of people raised the same concerns: Why give it to an
outsider? Shouldn't it be handled by someone inside?

At the time, I thought I had two answers to that:

First, although the Conversation FSM was crucial, it was also something of a stand-alone app that I could easily hand to someone else. All
the other work I did was inexorably intertwined with everyone else's
projects. I couldn't easily give the API app to someone else, because
they'd also have to learn all about Hwan's iPhone app, and I couldn't
easily ask someone else to work on the Salesforce app, because they'd
have to understand Sital's NLP app. But the Conversation FSM was a
standalone project.

Second, I was hoping Gregory would replace Sital and thus become an
insider.

Tuesday, September 15th, 2015

The board of directors would be meeting in two days. John felt it was crucial that we have a working demo, and he sent us the following email:

> Urgent plan sechedule. LeaseLet me know where we're atnd what kind of timeline we loooking at.
>
> 1) Sital fix Model
> 1) Add-in Sital's latet
> 2) Make s message fm phone creates oppportunity n Salesforce
> 3) Give John 4 hours to test the it and put in in thouh ringer
> 4) Demo

I was worried about number three (which was actually the fourth item in the list). What if we found a bug that we needed a week to fix? John had repeatedly promised this software to the board without leaving any buffer for dealing with serious upsets—and all summer we had only known serious upsets (as well as radical redefinitions of the company which were forced upon us by the Board of Directors).

I got to the office at 11:00 A.M. John arrived around 2:00 P.M. I asked him, "What happens if we don't have this working on the seventeenth?"

I am not exaggerating when I say that John's eyes went wide with terror. "We have to have this working on the seventeenth!"

"But what if we don't?"

"We *have* to have this working on the seventeenth!" he repeated fervently.

I was worried by that response. "What will the board of directors do if this is not working on the seventeenth?"

"Why would this not work on the seventeenth?" It seemed as if there was no way he could entertain that possibility.

"I am asking a hypothetical question." I thought it was obvious, but I was willing to emphasize the fictional nature of the scenario if it would calm him down.

"But why would you ask that?" The intensity of his reaction was as if I'd just asked him something obscene.

"Because I think hypothetical questions are important."

"I don't! I think *working* is important! Let's work hard and get this software running!"

"I'm sure we'll get it working at some point, but we have already seen

77

many unexpected delays." I pointed this out as calmly as I possibly could. "What if we encounter another?"

"If we miss this deadline, I'm going to ask you to talk to Milburn."

He threatened this as if it were the worst punishment he could imagine inflicting on me. Like, if the prisoner does not break during waterboarding, then we have them talk to Milburn.

"You don't want to talk to him?" I treaded carefully. "You talk to him every day."

"No, you can talk to him about this."

I was wary. It sounded a lot like I was being set up to take the fall for John's bad decisions. A part of me very much wanted to talk to the board, just to be sure they understood the real situation. I wanted to warn them about Sital. I wanted to impress upon them the absolute urgency of the Conversation FSM. But I didn't want my first real conversation with Milburn to be dominated by the question, "Why are you running late?"

I worried that the board had no real idea what was going on. Would there ever come a moment when John simply said to Milburn, "We need another month"? It seemed John lacked that kind of courage. I was unable to imagine him saying, "We can't build a stable system without the Conversation FSM, and that is at least a month away, since we have not yet hired anyone to work on it."

WEDNESDAY, SEPTEMBER 16TH, 2015

John wrote:

> *Milburn stilll asking ETA of EVERYTHING 100% finished andusable annd deploy. So any estimatee wood be nice, rather be conservative thn aggressivend telll them another dae that we miss. Thanks*

I wasn't sure what "everything 100% finished" referred to. Back in June we had agreed that building the full iPhone app would take at least six months. Then we had thrown that away and started over, but we had not generated a new estimate for what it would take to build a pure NLP interface for all of Salesforce. I assumed that would take at least a six months to a year from where we were now. But I think he was asking about something much more limited than that.

I responded:

You would need to define this strictly. Last Thursday we were able to get a message from the user to Salesforce, but there were many problems. There will be serious rough edges for several more weeks, especially regarding how much a user can say before our ability to track conversations breaks down. So it's really a question of how many rough edges you are willing to tolerate.

John responded with a list that made sense for a demo:

100% usable:
I can sen message frm iPhone
App confrms confrms results from nlp
I can confirm
It creates a new oppotunity in Salesforce correct data i corrrect areass
***if a required field is missing, it will ask f field then askto confirm everything

This left out any kind of error handling, but it was a sufficient list for a simple demo.

I tried to articulate what might have been the absolute minimum that would allow us to move forward:

On the subject of "if a required field is missing, prompt the user for the missing field"—this is exactly the kind of thing that needs to be handled by the FSM, but we might be able to use some hack to create the illusion that this basically works. On other issues, such as the Salesforce integration, I need about ten days. I am pleased to think that the NLP is now stable, so I can now finally focus on Salesforce integration.

I later learned that John told the board that everything would be done in ten days, meaning the twenty-sixth. Which is not what I had said. I had said that we would be facing serious rough edges for several more weeks. I did think the Salesforce integration would be done in ten days. But clearly, a panic had taken hold somewhere, and John, or Milburn, no longer wanted to hear nuanced estimates. They were desperate to have something working.

I should have repeated that the system would not be stable until the Conversation FSM was done, but I felt like I had already repeated this so many times that I would be insulting their intelligence if I said it even once more. Then again, panic has nothing to do with intelligence.

Unknown to me, John began scheduling meetings with investors and customers with the twenty-sixth in mind.

I have worked at many places where an app gets a month of testing before it is revealed to the public. It's a setup for disappointment to promise customers a working app when the app is still rapidly evolving every day.

John and I stayed at the office till 2:00 A.M. I finally got the whole system working, so we could send a message from the iPhone, to the API, then to the NLP, then parse it correctly, then send it back to the iPhone for confirmation, and then send it to Salesforce. The whole thing was ridiculously fragile and would remain so till the Conversation FSM was done. The illusion was there, though, and we could use the illusion for a demo.

Thursday, September 17th, 2015

John met with the board of directors and showed them our demo. They were delighted. Apparently he never told them that the whole thing was an illusion. Or maybe he told them and Milburn disregarded the information. I'll never know.

John also discussed hiring Gregory, and apparently the board approved it. Unknown to me, Gregory was only being offered a two-week contract, during which he would have to prove himself. Because of our delays (two weeks had passed since we first spoke with him), Gregory had accepted another full-time job. Still, he was willing to work with us part time. This was not ideal, but it was what we had to live with.

Friday, September 18th, 2015

On some level, all of us had been adapting to the weaknesses in Sital's code. Because it was fragile, we tended to use nicely constructed sentences whenever we tested it. In the real world, however, users would inevitably write a lot of nonsense—colloquialisms, slang, abbreviations and shorthand from the world of texting—so I again tried to test it with that degree of nonsense.

> I jus sol a mil a that shit to Carol .... 10000/week delivery for a year

And once again, the NLP app crashed. I found Sital on Slack. I pointed out to him that even if the user did make a mistake, his app should not crash. Instead, the response should always be something that makes sense to the user, such as "Sorry, we didn't understand what you meant" or something more specific, such as, "Please tell us the name of your customer."

Back in July I had spent a week creating a testing app that fired weird sentences at his app, and it made sure the NLP app always gave the result we expected. That had given us a guarantee that his code was stable. Unfortunately, my app was written back when his app was supposed to give a simple response to a single sentence. My testing app was now obsolete. I wanted Sital to create something similar, adapted to the reality that we now wanted our software to handle entire conversations. He promised he would work on this.

And to his credit, he did. Over the next few weeks he learned how to write "unit tests," and he built a suite of automated tests that could find weaknesses in his code. He was slowly learning how to be a real computer programmer.

I didn't know that on September 18, though. What I did know was that I had spent months asking him to emphasize stability in his code, and he had failed to do so.

I wrote to John:

> I am frustrated that I still need to write Sital these reminders in September. As if the need for error correction is not obvious to anyone who has studied computer science.

And he responded:

> You and I will sit dwn for 15 minutes monday and diicuss our plan to start interviewng new people right awy.We will findd someon good

Monday, September 21st, 2015

John postponed the conversation about Sital. Apparently we had other things to focus on.

Gregory started working nights with us. He was saving up to buy a house for himself, his girlfriend, and their daughter, so he was willing to give us all his nights and weekends. He had a fantastic amount of energy. I can't imagine working as hard as he worked, and for multiple companies too.

There were many things that impressed me about Gregory, but I think the single best thing about him was that he never lost his sense of humor. There were a lot of nights when we were still working at midnight, and he probably got up at 7:00 A.M. for his other job, yet he never showed any sign of tiredness or stress. He just kept making good suggestions and writing good code. In most respects, he was a better programmer than I was.

I started working on "nlp-converter," a new app that would take over most of the work previously handled by our NLP engine. As much as possible, I wanted to reduce the number of technologies that Sital needed to understand: concurrency, Redis, JSON serialization.

The nlp-converter was written in Clojure, so now all of the apps on the server were written in the same language (Sital's code was in Java, but his code was no longer an independent app, it was now a library that lived inside of the nlp-converter). This eliminated a whole category of problems for us. I wish I'd done this sooner, but of course, in the chaos of the moment, under the pressure of time, it's often difficult to know which decisions will have the biggest payoff.

One problem we faced was integrating all of the work. I set up a wiki on GitHub and established two pages for each app: one that showed what data the app expected to receive, and one that showed what data it returned. I emphasized to everyone the importance of keeping these pages up to date.

John apparently told Sital that he should ignore the wiki, because documentation was a long-term issue that delayed us from achieving our short-term goals. Possibly it did, but as I had said to Hwan all summer, we could not continue to be in crisis forever. There had to come some moment when we focused on long-term issues, so that when the future arrived it would not be a crisis.

Tuesday, September 22nd, 2015

I took the train to DC John was in the nation's capital visiting family. Gregory was also there visiting, mainly to help his girlfriend pack up her stuff after graduation, so he took time off from his regular job to join us at WeWork. And obviously Hwan was there. So we had this one day where almost the whole team was in DC—John, Gregory, Hwan, and I. The only person left in New York was Sital.

Much of the day was focused on bringing Gregory up to speed. He had spent the whole previous week studying FSMs, so he was able to discuss this issues with me with reasonable technical detail.

We decided to get a pizza for lunch.

What happened next was a revelation.

There was a popular pizza place about ten blocks away, so we decided to walk. We got about halfway, then ran into a red light and stopped to wait.

Some moments strike us with such a clarifying force that we remember them with amazing detail. I recall there was a mother standing to my right, with a very small child, and she was trying to get the child to stop crying. There was a homeless man to my left, leaning against a parking sign. It was a warm day and the sun was bright in the sky. An attractive woman in red shorts ran by.

It was an ordinary moment, banal. Four men walking down a street to get pizza. It was the kind of moment when people let their guard down. The kind of moment when liars forget to lie.

John smiled and pointed down one of the side streets.

"Hey look!" he blurted. "That's where it all started. That's where I did my internship with Milburn."

My head turned slowly in John's direction. I was amazed by what I had just heard, but I disguised my shock.

"You worked for Milburn?" I asked.

"Yes, last summer. That's where I learned about Salesforce. That's where we came up with the idea for Celolot."

He had told a thousand lies to hide the origins of Celolot, and now he unthinkingly revealed the truth. The idea that he and Dennis and Griffin had founded Celolot and then gone to a Salesforce conference and magically lucked into investors who immediately wrote them a check for $1.3 million—all of that had seemed too good to be true. This was so much more credible: that he'd been working with Milburn, that the two of them birthed the idea of the company, that Milburn invested, and that he then lined up some of his friends as investors. Or maybe Milburn didn't have any money to invest at all; maybe he simply used his skills as a salesperson to rope in some suckers.

Or perhaps Milburn had come up with the whole idea on his own. As a freelance contractor, I have, many times, had a client with these characteristics:

- Middle aged and wealthy
- Comes up with an idea for software/website
- Assumes it will be easy
- Doesn't have time to work on it themselves, so assigns it to their assistant
- Checks in often, but leaves the details to the assistant
- Is incredulous when the project takes longer than expected, assumes the assistant is incompetent
- Yells at assistant, tells them to stop being lazy
- Assistant then yells at whoever was hired to work on the task

It occurred to me that Celolot might easily be another example of that same pattern. In that case, Milburn was the real CEO of the company, and John was simply his assistant. That would explain the daily phone calls.

Up to a point I can sincerely admire Milburn. What he'd envisioned so far was a classic example of what Peter Drucker had defined as an innovation based on "process need." He describes it in *Innovation and Entrepreneurship*:

> *Process need, unlike the other sources of innovation, does not start out with an event in the environment, whether internal or external. It starts out with the job to be done. It is task-focused rather than situation-focused. It perfects a process that already exists, replaces a link that is weak, redesigns an existing old process around newly available knowledge. In innovations that are based on process need, everybody in the organization always knows that the need exists. Yet usually no one does anything about it. However, when the innovation appears, it is immediately accepted as "obvious" and soon becomes "standard."*[7]

Milburn had started with a task: tracking the sales process. He was aware of the "weak link": salespeople hated using the complicated CRMs, such as Salesforce. He used new knowledge to envision a solution: NLP would make it painless for salespeople to use the big CRMs. Companies wasted millions on software that no one liked to use, and so Celolot was the answer to an urgent process need.

To give him the credit he is due, Milburn had been ahead of the curve on this one. But he can rightly be criticized for the weaknesses of his execution. All over the world, there were probably thousands of startups looking to use NLP to solve various business problems. The winners would be the ones that were best at turning an idea into reality. If we didn't get our act together, then companies such as Tactile.com would walk away with the prize.

WEDNESDAY, SEPTEMBER 23RD, 2015

John had been working with an outside agency to develop the video that we would be posting on our promotional web site. The video was extremely impressive. It promised many features that I thought we would need another six months to develop, but if the goal of the video was to simply to sound impressive—after all, maybe it was more aimed at investors than customers—then it was very well done.

THURSDAY, SEPTEMBER 24TH, 2015

Since I learned that John had done an internship with Milburn, I was curious to learn more about the situation. Clearly I had been lied to. But what was the truth?

There wasn't much about Milburn online, but I looked over his LinkedIn profile, and I looked up the companies that he had been active with. Lying comes naturally to great salespeople, so I wasn't surprised that he'd been successful in that field. But what did that really mean?

A great salesperson has a repertoire of psychological tricks. They can make you their friend, or they can make you feel guilt; they know when to offer a compliment; they also know how to disguise a negative comment as a neutral observation and thus undercut the confidence of their prey.

Milburn's career had apparently done especially well during the 1990s. I wondered if he was now feeling stuck. Stagnancy in middle age leads to all kinds of wild adventures—usually an affair or an expensive car—but perhaps it was Milburn's style to try to launch a business. Anything to revive that old feeling of success.

Apparently he was also somewhat technical. He'd learned Microsoft Excel in the 1990s, and he knew some VisualBasic. Perhaps he'd written some VBA code and connected some Excel spreadsheets to some databases. He knew more about computers than the average salesperson. From the sounds of it, he knew exactly enough to be a disaster.

Friday, September 25th, 2015

John had scheduled a meeting with potential customers, but the software was not working reliably yet. He scheduled another meeting for the twenty-eighth, and the twenty-ninth, and the thirtieth. All of these eventually had to be cancelled. The whole team was working long hours to transform our demo into real working code, but it was an arduous effort. I tried several times to hard-code enough stuff that might have worked as a demo, but there were always edge cases that raised errors.

John grew frustrated. He reminded me that on August 30 I had promised to have everything done by September 10. I explained that I had only been talking about the demo. He then said that on the sixteenth I had promised that I'd be done in ten days. I insisted that I had only said that I needed ten days for the Salesforce integration. He complained that none of my estimates were accurate. I reminded him that we had had a working demo on September 17. He said it was too fragile and it broke easily. I insisted it was a demo, not a real product. He repeated that I had promised that everything would be done. I said I had promised the demo would be done. He said that I had done a bad job of communicating the state of the software. I suggested that he was hearing what he wanted to hear.

I wanted to go to DC one day a week so I could work directly with Hwan, but I was told we could not afford it. I was extremely frustrated when he told me this, especially since I didn't think it was true.

"We will soon have enough money to hire Arthur full-time, but we don't have enough money for me to go to DC?" I asked, suspicious.

John repeated that we didn't have enough money for a train ticket. Possibly he was cutting off my funds as some kind of petty revenge for what he felt were my inaccurate estimates. If so, he was sabotaging the whole project for the sake of keeping me and Hwan from working together.

On the other hand, maybe they really were running out of money. What had happened to that next round of investment that he had felt so confident about?

Tuesday, September 29th, 2015

John was out meeting with people, but he checked in with me on Slack.

John

Juts checking in againon status, i realized were bit pushed back. Just a reminder we do not need existing opps today. Also, do not worry at all about products, event, or anything lse Salesforce. We just need to be able to create new opps, and have accounts/contact list. We just need to launch already, hope we're nit being stalled out on time working on products, events, or existing opps right now. Milburn is anxious. Let me know how everything is coming along.

I had the impression that Milburn must have risked his own reputation when he decided on the Big Pivot. That would put him in a bad situation now. Was the board of directors angry with him? In retrospect it seemed obvious that we should have finished the traditional iPhone app that we'd been working on—we could have launched with that in August and called it "Version 1.0." Big cheers for the team! Champagne for everyone! Our first customers! Our first sales! A party to celebrate!

Then we could have done the Big Pivot and focused on our experimental Conversation app, and that would have been Version 2.0. If Milburn had consulted the tech team back at the end of July, then we might have been able to have that discussion. But Milburn had made the decision on his own and sold it to the rest of the board. The tech team was never consulted. And now he was "anxious."

I recalled what John had said back on July 28: "We need to go faster!"

At the time I was confused—how would it help us go faster if we threw away our code and engaged in a wild experiment that no tech company had yet gotten right? Assuming that the decision had come from Milburn, he had a hell of a lot to answer for. I could imagine that a lot of the investors who had trusted him with money were now feeling like he had lied to them.

Friday, October 2nd, 2015

We had taken away almost all of Sital's responsibilities. We kept him around to work on the NLP library, but until we had our first customers and could test with real-world data, there was not much to do. John asked Sital to edit what would be our first newsletter. I found this surprising.

Sital completed the assignment and posted his work to Google Docs. It was confusing and very badly written, much like his Java code. I was pretty disturbed by the fact that John and Milburn were engaged in this effort to make artificial work for Sital.

"When do we get rid of Sital?" Hwan asked me on a brief phone call.

"I don't know."

"It's been three weeks."

"I know."

"Should we talk to John again?"

"I think we might have to."

I told John that Hwan and I wanted to talk to have a phone conference with him. Late that afternoon, we went into a conference room. We told Sital that we were going to discuss API issues that did not affect him, so he did not need to attend.

Once again, Hwan was very polite. He was always more diplomatic than I was. He raised the question of when Sital would leave. John suggested that we needed Sital for a while longer. Hwan was concerned about the number of delays that Sital had caused.

John said, "Listen, the last time the board of directors met, we had one slide up on the screen, and all it said was *Sital?* with a big question mark. So the board has considered it. But here's the thing: we're an NLP startup. We need to raise money from investors. The board feels we can't get more money unless we have an NLP expert on the staff."

"But can't we get a real NLP expert?" I asked. "Like, one who actually knows how to write computer code?"

"That will be easier once we raise more money," he explained. "Then we can offer someone a bigger salary."

"So we have to wait till we get more money?"

"That's the best option."

"Do you know when you will raise more money?" I asked.

"Just a few more weeks." He sounded confident. "We will have the money soon."

"How can you be so sure?" I asked.

"We know." He seemed exasperated by my doubts. "It's guaranteed. We've got a VC firm that definitely wants to invest."

"You can never be sure about that," I said.

"We are sure," he bragged. "Pretty sure. Very sure."

"But you can never really be sure," I repeated. "Didn't you expect the money in September? And now it's October."

"Okay, okay, okay, okay!" He was tired of arguing with me. "Assume we get the money next week. Can we deal with Sital then?"

"Sure," I said. "If we get the money next week. But are we going to get the money next week?"

"Don't worry about it!" he insisted. "This money is guaranteed."

"I sure hope that is true."

I am sometimes innocent when it comes to corporate politics, so I was slow to appreciate what I had just been told. The Celolot board of directors had formally considered Sital and formally kept him, so now their credibility would be tied to Sital—and in fact, from this point forward, any criticism of Sital could be considered criticism of the board.

Months would pass before I fully appreciated the legal implications of this. If the board raised money as an NLP startup, with Sital as their NLP expert, then they had to believe in Sital to accept investments in good faith. If the board felt there were serious problems with Sital but still asked investors for money, wouldn't that constitute selling equity in bad faith?

Sunday, October 4th, 2015

John wrote via email:

Hey Lawrence just cheking backin, as y said you'd have a good feel of a good feel things and wrapping up by sunday. Just shoot me pdate, thanks

I replied:

I am still working on integration issues. About Gregory: if he is looking for more to do, he should move ahead and think about additional subjects that we will want to soon incorporate.

John wrote back:

lets discuss tomrow in person need to set a plan with him. What time will you be in tomorrow? Also, any update on a for finish or still up in t air?

I wrote all this without knowing that our first contract with Gregory had come to an end. But then Gregory CC'd me when he wrote to John:

We will need to close out the first consulting contract and open a new one for a week to week part time position before I start the work mentioned above. Once we get these details finished then I will hop right into it.

I was angry when I realized that our initial contract with Gregory had been so limited. I was getting pressure to move faster, yet there was this huge piece of work that needed to be done—the Conversation FSM—and despite multiple conversations and emails and warnings, I had not convinced John how crucial it was. Or maybe I had convinced John, but he had been unable to convince Milburn.

I found it especially frustrating that Gregory had to prove himself, whereas Sital did not.

I wrote to John:

I believe that Celolot will move faster if we fire Sital and make Gregory our data scientist. He's demonstrated great speed and skill. Please note that Sital had all of August to figure out a way to manage the state of the user conversations, and he failed, whereas Gregory built the basics of a system in a week.

John replied:

Wel sit dwn and have big catch up about Gregory, Sital, vacation, etc. tomorrow as soon as everything s fixed and wrapped up.

Monday, October 5th, 2015

John was at the incubator in the morning. I worked with Sital to fix the communication between his app and the other apps.

John made a big show of being frustrated. He sighed heavily. He would stand up, move things around on his desk, sit down again, ask if we were ready to test. Our answer was always the same: no, we were not ready. We were trying to track down a bug.

Finally, John left. He had meetings elsewhere in the city. Every hour he wrote us on Slack to ask if we were done. I always gave the same reply: no, we were not done.

Sital left at 5:00 P.M. to go to the gym. After the gym he went home, and then later that night he reached out on Slack to let me know he was working.

As the night rolled on, the incubator emptied out. Varak and Perrino ordered pizza. The RavenCart crew ordered Mexican food. Surprisingly, Vladimir was not with them. By midnight, we were the only four startups that were still working.

The fifth ended and the sixth began, but no one noticed.

Tuesday, October 6th, 2015

At 1:00 A.M., John wrote to me on Slack.

John
hows everything coming along// whats the latest?

lkrubner
I am still working on integration issues.

Around 2:00 A.M., the tech crew of RavenCart got up and left.

I worked until 3:00 A.M., then decided to go to sleep. Before quitting for the night, I wrote an email to the entire team:

1.) the nlp is now much slower than it used to be. Whereas response times used to be 3 seconds or less, response times are now more like 20 seconds.

2.) the Conversation FSM needs to be tweaked so its clear how to advance from one state to the next state. For instance, in the old days, once I was happy with the data, I would write 'yes' in response to the question "Can you confirm that this is what you want in Salesforce?" and the 'yes' would trigger a write to Salesforce. We need to agree on what text will trigger a Salesforce write.

John wrote back instantly:

Ok, but its alll finally working finally and we can relase it tomoow correct?

We were not even close to being done.
I wrote back:

I have not yet tried to create an Opportunity with the new code. Some changes to the Conversation FSM will be necessary before that is even possible.

This was John's reply:

Whether it finished or not. We are releasing tomorrw Speed NEEDS TO STOP being worried about, what exactly user needs to respnd with "yes" etc. NEEDS TO STOP being worried about, getting everything perfect NEEDS TO STOP being worried about. We just NEED to launch. Its tht simple. I don't think you guys are understanding betas and test do not care at all if its perfect, whole point of a pilot, beta, etc is to give the them something to test, not cotinually delay anddelay. So again, we re handing out usable version tomrrow.

If the software didn't work, then what would we release? We could offer the demo we had working on September 17, but he seemed to want a real working app.
Then he sent another email:

Aand not late ate tomorrow night, i mean tomrow around lunch/early afternoon

I want a billion dollars, but just because I want a billion dollars doesn't mean I will get them. Likewise, he might want working software the next day, but simply wanting it did not mean he would get it.

We were now running into the situation that I had warned about all summer: we had burned up our runway with unnecessary delays and suddenly felt like we had no room left for takeoff.

I wrote back to John and told him I would try my best the next day. Of course, I always tried my best, so that was meaningless. Could anyone think of a way to make this work before the Conversation FSM for the Conversations was working? I had a half-dozen ideas that I was willing to try, but none of them were certain. It was like being told that I had to build a working car by tomorrow, but the guy who was working on the engine was only part time and would not be done for another month.

I wanted to sleep on the couch in the back of the office, but I went back there and saw that Varak was already asleep there. That was the best spot to sleep in the office. I ended up sleeping on the couches in the middle of the office, but they were rotten places to sleep because people came in and out of the office all night long.

Over the course of several nights, I realized that the lead developer for the "apply-NLP-techniques-to-legal-documents" startup, Voice of Law, often arrived at 7:00 A.M. When I slept in back I never heard him come in, but when I slept on the couches in the middle of the office, whenever he showed up and started working was when I would get up and start working too. I couldn't sleep when there was someone clattering on their keyboard just thirty feet away from me.

On those occasions when I slept on the couch in the back of the office, I was often able to sleep straight from 3:00 A.M. to 8:00 A.M., and the only interruption was at 6:00 A.M. when the cleaning crew came through and grabbed the garbage. But on those occasions when I slept on the couches in the middle of the office, I don't think I ever got more than thirty straight minutes of sleep.

At 4:00 A.M., God knows why, a guy and a girl came into the office, sat at a desk, and ate a vegan meal. I know it was vegan because the guy kept asking, "You're sure this is vegan?" and the girl kept saying, "Yes, it's vegan." I believe they were new hires working with Daniel and Svetlana. Or they were co-founders and they had been in a different country and had only recently been allowed into the U.S. Why they had to eat a vegan meal at the incubator at 4:00 A.M. will forever escape me. When they were done, the guy pulled some clothes out of a backpack and put some clothes in another backpack, and then they left with the backpack.

At 5:00 A.M., Vladimir came in, sat at his desk, and began banging on his keyboard very urgently. I could not imagine why he was here so early. Maybe he felt bad that he had not been here with the rest of his team. I also had the impression that RavenCart was in bad financial trouble, but I didn' see how that justified showing up at 5:00 A.M. and disturbing my sleep.

Vladimir sometimes played League of Legends with Varak and Perrino. I had never joined them, knowing I'd be a terrible teammate given the investment of time required to be adept, but sometimes I watched. I had gotten to know Vladimir a bit from the late-night game sessions.

I got up and I went over to him. He looked up at me and laughed.

"Late night?" he asked.

"Early morning?" I asked.

He pointed at a white board behind me. I looked around and saw the words written, "We will handle one million transactions by December 1."

I turned back to face him and asked, "Will you handle one million transactions by December 1?"

He looked pained. Then he shrugged. Then he went back to typing.

"I wish you luck," I said.

I went to check the couch in back and Varak was still sleeping. The bastard. I liked him, but I also needed to sleep.

I returned to the couches in the middle of the office. The cleaning crew came through at 6:00 A.M. and woke me up. Thankfully, they also woke up Varak. He decided to go to his desk and start working. I walked over to the couch where he had been sleeping and lay down. It was quiet in back. I was able to sleep until 8:00 A.M., when the office got loud enough that I couldn't sleep anymore.

Then I went to my desk and started in where I'd left off at 3:00 A.M. Various ideas seemed possible, but I could not find one that worked. Around noon John sent an email:

I'm 5 minutes away so let's be ready to push our first usable relase live

Well, yes, it would be great to have a usable release live, but first we had to come up with software that actually worked. I wrote to Gregory and told him that I liked everything that I had seen from him so far, and that I wanted his help cleaning up the NLP code that Sital had written. I had not yet told Gregory about the complicated politics regarding Sital. As far as he knew, we were all very happy working together.

I wrote to Gregory:

I am sorry to say I have not had the time to give Sital the kind of feedback that might help him refine the NLP app. I think he would benefit if an experienced programmer helped him abstract and refactor the code, mostly to make the code more re-usable, but also for performance reasons.

Gregory wrote back:

94

I will dive into Sital's code this evening (pending an agreement with John). A video chat would be a good way for me to discover what he has done so far.

The "pending an agreement with John" reminded me exactly how much John was sabotaging the project. Why exactly should I work all night if John refused to hire the programmer I wanted to hire and he refused to fire the programmer I wanted to fire?

I wrote John to remind him of the many times I'd told him that the Conversation FSM was crucial and we need someone working on it. John responded that Celolot should not take on any new obligations until we had a working app.

I was furious, but I did my best to respond politely. There were so many times I felt like a broken record during my months at Celolot. I simply wrote:

Gregory has done a fantastic job thus far, and a working FSM that can handle conversations is crucial to what we do. We need to keep him working with us as much as possible.

John still waited a few days before finalizing a contract with Gregory. John seemed to think that he was punishing me for not finishing a working system, but of course, the system could not really work without a functioning FSM that could keep track of our conversations. That was what Milburn committed us to when he committed us to the Big Pivot. I had explained this many times, but somehow the reality of the situation was being ignored. It was possible that John understood the situation, but Milburn did not.

I wanted to get out of the office. I called Michael and arranged to meet him for lunch. I had moved to New York City in 2009, and Michael moved up the following year. Like all people who'd been through some shared trauma, we had a lot of inside jokes that would set us laughing—"Archaeomediaology," for example, or "Our software will put you, our customer, in the driver's seat of real-time conscious human evolution." No other explanation was needed.

We met at B Cup Cafe, over on Avenue B in the East Village—not far from Quintessence, in fact. We jumped right into talking about the recent drama at Celolot; I explained that I was trying to transform a raw beginner into an experienced programmer, all while facing crisis-driven deadlines. I told him about the night of July 2, when we worked twenty-three straight hours in an attempt to be ready for our demo.

"What crazy hours you work!" he exclaimed. "I hope you're hourly!"

I shook my head. "Salary."

"Well, no one ever accused you of being smart."

"That's true."

"Whatever you're doing, it must be very important—because we have a free market system, and investors in our free system invested in your firm freely, proving that whatever you're doing is important."

"I'm all for free," I said.

"You know what makes the free market system so great?" he posed.

"Ego-driven investment by out-of-touch incompetents who assume their ignorance about an opportunity means they must be uniquely qualified to develop a solution?" I offered.

"Efficiency."

"I always guess the wrong answer."

"It's all about efficiency," he explained. "Lots of smart people have written about this. Big books. Huge books. Books full of smart. So you can go on believing whatever ridiculous nonsense you want to believe, but I admonish you: without the free market, your life would be empty and meaningless."

"Michael, have you ever worked at a successful startup?"

"Sure, lots of times," he boasted.

"Really?" I was genuinely surprised. "Twitter? Facebook? Uber? AirBnB? Where did you work?"

"XugarPoppsNow. ZeitgiestyInfinite. NefartitiWowYum."

"I've never heard of those."

"They're all bankrupt now," he said with a shrug.

"Wait, what's your definition of a successful startup?"

"Goes at least two years before declaring bankruptcy." He said it like it was obvious. "The soft bigotry of low expectations is your friend, Lawrence. I get to tell myself I'm having a fantastic career. It's the only way I can sleep at night." He grinned. "Otherwise it's back to the Ambien."

"I should try Ambien," I said. "Might help me get past my honesty problem, too."

"Ambien is a good start," he said. "But for real results, combine it with alcohol."

"How much alcohol?"

"Do you need to wake up?"

"Not personally, but my mom would be upset," I said.

"It's a tyranny they hold over us."

"Those who loved us first and loved us best?"

"The problem is they still do."

"Parents!" I agreed. "So annoying!"

For all our complaining, we were both the type that enjoyed our work, no matter how crazy it was. After lunch, we went back to our respective projects.

I spent the day responding to requests from Hwan and Sital. Since my apps were what connected everything, when any of the other programmers made changes to the messages they were sending, I needed to make matching changes.

Around 11:00 P.M., I went home. I couldn't sleep over at the office two nights in a row.

WEDNESDAY, OCTOBER 7TH, 2015

I woke up at 9:00 A.M. and checked my email. John had written me:

need to test t now. Somthing needs to be upladed I don't care what. N now

John was lucky that the project itself was exciting. Working on something so original and new was tremendous fun. I'm fairly sure that Hwan and Gregory felt something similar to what I did. Our loyalty was to the project, we had no loyalty to John. In my experience it is rare to get the chance to work on anything as interesting as this. The pressure John applied would have inspired a rebellion if the project itself had been less intriguing.

I wrote back to explain that we were still working on the code. He wrote back with exactly the same message, typos and all, so I assume he simply copy-and-pasted the text:

need to test t now. Somthing needs to be upladed I don't care what. N now

Okay, fine. I pushed all of the newest code to the server. At this point, we had a dozen apps. Some of these were minor and did background administrative stuff. We currently had six apps that were crucial: the iPhone app, the API app, the NLP app, the Salesforce app, the Salesforce login app, and the Conversation FSM.

None of these apps was perfect, but four out of the six basically worked. The Salesforce app and the Conversation FSM still needed some more attention.

Apparently John had tried to send a message from his iPhone and had gotten no response from the server. He was pissed.

John
not workkking

lkrubner
That is correct.

I got to the office at 11:00 A.M. John was out at some meetings, as usual. Sital was there, and he looked worried. He asked me if he could do anything to help. I said no. Then he asked what would happen if we didn't get the system working soon. I told him that I didn't know.

John came in around noon. He ostentatiously sent another message from his iPhone, even though there had been no changes since his earlier test. He again told me that the system was not working, and I again told him he was correct. He was furious about this, but he remained silent. He sat in his chair and stared at us. An hour later he tried to send yet another message from his iPhone.

It was childish. I still had not pushed any changes to the server, so we all knew that it wouldn't work. But he did it anyway, and then he told us that the system still wasn't working. I told him yet again that he was correct.

I had never before worked in such a tense environment.

John sat there for another hour doing almost nothing. He looked miserable. Sital looked worried, and he stayed focused on writing unit tests that would ensure the stability of his system. To his credit, Sital was becoming a real computer programmer. At the rate he was going, it was possible that by the summer of 2017 he would be everything we'd needed in the summer of 2015.

Milburn called John. I heard John say to the phone, "It isn't working." I couldn't hear exactly what Milburn was saying, but it was clear he was screaming. John winced at the rage and went back to the conference room. I wondered what would happen when he came out, whether he would actually have something to say to us or just sit there and stare some more.

I decided I wanted dinner. I also decided I would work from home for the rest of the evening. I could not tolerate any more of John staring at me.

I gathered my computer and bag and headed out. As I passed the door of the conference room where John was in a video chat with Milburn, I heard Milburn's voice.

"You made a mess, John, you made a mess. Again. You always screw things up, always. I give you a second chance and you screw it up. How many times have you screwed up this project? Listen, I tried to help you because your dad is my best friend, but look at what you've done. Look at what you've done. Do you know how this makes me feel? Do you understand how betrayed I feel? Do you remember that time when you were nine years old and we went camping, and you wanted to go out on the rocks in the river, and me and your dad said no, they're slippery, don't go out there, you'll get hurt. But you just had to do it. You had to do it. You wouldn't listen to us. You went out there on the rocks and you got hurt and then we had to take you to the hospital and our whole vacation was ruined. We could have had a nice time but you ruined it for everyone. And that's what you're doing now, you're ruining it for everyone."

There were several moments where John started to say something, but in every case Milburn talked over him. I wasn't sure who the guilty party was. Milburn wanted John to think that the current situation was John's fault, but was it? One of the fundamental problems was the chaos caused by the Big Pivot of July 28. As far as I could tell, that had been Milburn's decision, but apparently Milburn did not want to take responsibility for his mistakes. He was trying to put a massive guilt trip on John instead, and it seemed that John was not fighting back.

I walked home. If Milburn had known John since he was nine years old, then Milburn had had many years to plan for the moment when John would intern for him. I felt bad for John. He was twenty-two and he may have walked into a trap that had been years in the making.

Why come up with a fake origin story about Dennis and Griffin? It took me many weeks to figure that part out, but eventually I decided it was for the investors. After all, if you're an investor, which of these sounds more appealing:

1.) Some tired sixty-year-old salesman has a part-time project involving sales software and he's put his twenty-two-year-old assistant in charge of it. Please invest $1.3 million.
2.) Three brilliant and ambitious college guys came up with a plan to disrupt the multi-billion dollar CRM industry with the hottest NLP technologies currently available. Please invest $1.3 million.

Where would you put your money?

THURSDAY, OCTOBER 8TH, 2015

Despite the fact that he had no contract with us, Gregory continued to research the type of NLP software we were building, and he sent us several great ideas for how to move forward. He engaged me and John in a conversation about whether it was possible to build a general-purpose NLP schema that could work for every possible customer.

John argued it wouldn't be possible because, for instance, a company that was focused on healthcare would use different jargon than a company that was focused on automobiles. Gregory suggested that we use a basic template that would cover the 80% of words that would be common to all companies. Then we would only need to specialize on the remaining twenty percent.

These were good ideas. Even better was how fast Gregory was learning: in the space of two weeks, he had absorbed almost all of what we had spent the summer figuring out. I sent John an email urging him to work out some kind of contract with Gregory.

Hwan was amazing as well. Although we were all feeling the pressure of time, he stayed calm, responded to every request with a can-do attitude, and did an excellent job articulating to everyone else exactly what he would need from them.

Despite the progress, John was enraged that we were not done. Around midnight he posted an angry message on Slack:

John
I was tld this was workng and ive also been told itll be ready today everyday for the last 2-3 weeks. the 'issue is that it doesnt work. just need to send messages i dont car about stabilty nd long run anymore, i cannot express it enoguh no one cares. very simple. Just need a minimal viable product. the long run stuff all means nothing if this gets continus to get "delaayed one more day" for more and more days. very simple just send simple json mesages thats all so i can use the product already. just upload som sort of simple buildlike such tomorrow. Everyone havea good night and plently of sleep and talk to you all tomorrow when we have a minimal viable product upa dn runing and deeliverable tomorrow.

There was a lot here that seemed completely beside the point. We were not having any trouble serializing and deserializing JSON. We had fixed those issues in August. And we were not doing any work on long-term issues, though he might have thought that our documentation on Github was a long-run effort with no short-term benefit. That was false. We needed that documentation in order to understand what to expect from each other's apps on a day-to-day basis.

I've known twenty-two-year-olds who possessed the maturity to run a business, and I had assumed that John was one of them because investors had trusted him with $1.3 million. But the events of the past few months had made clear that he was not in this category. In fact, it struck me that Milburn might have chosen John as his puppet because John was an unusually weak individual who would simply do as he was told.

Within the tech community people often make the observation that in Silicon Valley, startups are created by engineers who can listen to and understand other engineers, whereas in New York City, startups are created by businesspeople who then hire engineers but don't understand them. Some people claim that because of this, Silicon Valley will always be the more vibrant startup scene. I have never agreed, but I was worried that Celolot was on its way to becoming another anecdote that could be used to bolster this notion.

I responded on Slack.

lkrubner
My suggestion would be: If you have never tested the software yourself, then don't promise it to customers and don't schedule demos. Most of the places that I have worked have at least a month of testing before a product goes to the public. You are setting yourself up for failure if you promise software that isn't yet working—we can never be certain exactly what day it will be ready. And even if it is working, you should test it yourself to see if there are any serious bugs.

FRIDAY, OCTOBER 9TH, 2015

Because of the chronic sleep deprivation of the preceding weeks, I developed this peculiar protocol to ensure that I actually woke up in the morning. Before I went to sleep, I brewed some coffee and poured it into a mug. I put the mug on my bedside table. Then I set two alarms: one alarm for the time I need to be up, and another alarm for a half an hour prior to that. When the first alarm went off, I rolled over, barely conscious, and drank the entire mug of coffee, then fell back to sleep. That way the caffeine was in full force a half an hour later—coursing through my blood vessels on its way to the frontal lobe of my brain—when my second, real alarm went off. I truly don't know how I would've functioned many a morning had I not developed this technique.

I got to the office early. John was out at meetings, but I had no idea who he might be meeting with.

John wrote to me to tell me that the board of directors was running out of patience. We needed to get the software into the hands of customers soon, otherwise the board would cut off all funding and shut Celolot down.

I couldn't tell if he was telling the truth or making an empty threat. Either way, if the goal was to motivate us to work harder, it was an incredibly stupid move. The market for computer programmers was hot; I was sure I could find another job. I cared about Celolot because it was an unusual chance to work on an ambitious project, not because I was desperate for a paycheck.

I reminded John that if he wanted to see us move faster, he could fire Sital and hire a competent replacement. For some reason, this option was off the table.

John wrote to me:

Most likely not hiring Gregory so I ca hire somone good to come look at our strategyy clean all this up and get us polished for ASlesforce. My concern is gettting us acttually working without hard coding not some stability issue for Gregory to fix, which would be great, but not a priority at all. This isnt somthing I want to do and obviously hurts us but I'm given no choice. Were delayed almost 3 weeks, next board meeting we're supposed to give customer feedback which I can't even get because ca't give the prodct tocustomers.

Can anyone recall when President Kennedy told NASA, "I believe that this nation should commit itself to achieving the goal, before this decade is out, of landing a man on the moon and returning him safely to the earth. However, we should not waste any time building a rocket engine. That would be nice, but it is not a priority. We must focus on building the stuff at the pointy top of the ship, where the astronauts will be."

No, no one can recall that. That didn't happen, because it would have been ridiculous. But now we were being told nearly the same thing: that the Conversation FSM—which our entire product depended on and which leadership had committed us to in the Big Pivot—was "not a priority at all." I was truly astonished by that line. Perhaps that message came from Milburn? John was such a spineless puppet that he would accept whatever Milburn told him, even if it went against all the evidence in the world.

This email was also the first time I was told that the board of directors was expecting customer feedback at the next meeting. These deadlines were insane. John was aware how fragile the demo on September 17 had been. Who thought we could go from that to a working product, used by paying customers, in one month? I knew that John did not like to deliver bad news, so when the board asked him, "Can we hear customer feed-back at the next meeting?" John had probably told them exactly what they wanted to hear.

Another email from John:

We are bringng in a consultant, , a friend of th eboard. Hee will find the mistake in the architecture you created. And you should come t the next meeeeting, to tel the board why your software doessnt work.

Again, I would have loved to talk to the board about whom we should hire, whom we should fire, and how to move forward. But under the circumstances, it seemed like I was being asked to take responsibility for John's or Milburn's bad decisions.

I responded:

I'll consolidate my various emails into a single email for the consultant. The consultant can explain things to the board. You don't need me. Over the last two months I've made two suggestions regarding person-nel: fire Sital and hire Gregory. Over the last two months you've ignored those two suggestions. That's your decision and your responsibility. But don't ask me to explain our strategy to the board when the decisions are not mine.

John, or someone using John's account, wrote back:

Lawrence, I'm sorry to say that you have seriously misread the situa-tion. And I feel that you have misrepresented yourself. I am hurt by the implication that I have not listened to your requests. Quite the oppo-site, I feel that Celolot has gone to considerable lengths to cater to all of your demands. During the summer you wanted to visit DC, and we arranged to buy you train tickets so you could go to DC whenever you wished. Later, you demanded another programmer be put on the team, and almost immediately we leapt into action and brought someone else onto the team. If we have not always been able to indulge the specifics of each and every one of your ultimatums, that is only because our fi-nances are finite, and some difficult choices have needed to be made regarding our true priorities.

As to personnel, you and I sat down last week, on October 2nd, and discussed this issue at some length. We were in total agreement concerning Sital. He is a brilliantly creative data scientist of incredible genius, but we are at such an early stage, we have not been able to take full advantage of his astonishing skills. He is not what we need right now. If you want to start looking for Sital's replacement today, then I am happy to move forward with you, or we can wait and see if we raise another investor round quickly (and thus our budget for NLP would substantially increase). When we spoke, you agreed to wait. If you want to switch strategies, and not wait, I am still happy to support you in your decision. The ONLY thing that's changing is that we've decided to hire someone else with more experience than Gregory. The consultant that we now plan to bring in will still do all of Gregory's work, just as soon as he's able to fix the other problems with your architecture. I'm confused about what you have against this plan. It's the best of both worlds. You wanted an extra programmer on the team, and we will have one, but someone who is much more experienced than Gregory.

Once again, I was astounded. Everything about this email indicated that my words simply weren't getting through. Gregory had been doing great work, but we were getting rid of him. Sital was a creative genius. The problems we faced were not caused by Sital, nor by the lack of a Conversation FSM, but by some vague, yet-to-be-diagnosed problem with the architecture I had come up with. If we were in a court of law, and the court only reviewed the written documentation, then this message went a long way toward suggesting that all of the problems at the company were caused by me. Not by Sital, not by Milburn. Me.

And again, there was the distinctly noticeable characteristic that it was completely free of spelling errors and other typos.

Later, John sent some requests to Hwan, asking that the text appear differently on the iPhone when a user was editing their response. Hwan and I worked until 2:00 A.M., exchanging messages on Slack and implementing John's requested changes. I slept at the office, and since it was a Friday night, it was unusually quiet.

Saturday, October 10th, 2015

Buzzing fluorescent lights. Dry office air. Adjustable-height chairs. Cheaply-assembled desks. "All the conventions conspire to make this fort assume the furniture of home," Auden wrote, and I finally understood him: the fort had become my home. I had memorized everything in the office, even the distances. I could walk them with my eyes closed.

Because it was a Saturday, people trickled in late to work. I don't think a single person arrived at the office until after 9:00 A.M., and even at 10:00 A.M., there were only a dozen people there. Sleeping on the couch in the back, I was undisturbed until at least 9:30 A.M. This was the absolute best rest I ever got at the office.

I went downstairs and across the street to Essen, where I got some eggs, bread, and coffee. It was still warm, despite the lateness of the season. The sky was a brilliant blue, but the trees were changing color, and I felt that sadness of knowing the days of comfortable weather were coming to an end.

John had asked if I could get the system working. I had promised to make a good faith effort to try to hack something together. In retrospect, this was a mistake—as each time I promised to try something, he seemed to hear, "I guarantee 100% that I will get everything working." His desperation made him stupid. My attempts to educate him on the risks we were facing never got through his fear.

Since we had broken off our contract with Gregory, I would have to take full responsibility for writing the Conversation FSM. This would take a few weeks.

I drank more coffee, and then more coffee, and then more coffee. Towards the evening, I wrote to John on Slack.

lkrubner
I made progress today, but we are still facing weeks of work, rather than days of work.

John
We had working systm oon th 17, why dont we hav a system now?

lkrubner
We have the old demo. Is that all you need? Or do you need a stable system?

What he said next sounded like a threat.

John
Youu will need to tak fulll responsibilt for breking our system.

I decided the office had become poisonous to my health, and it would be best if I worked remotely for a few days. I took the subway to Penn Station, bought a train ticket for Charlottesville, Virginia, and left. I figured I would buy a change of clothes once I got down south. Actually, I realized I still had some clothes down there, in the closet at the apartment of a family friend.

Sunday, October 11th, 2015

Breakfast would be crepes. At the back of the Jefferson Theater, next to the Live Arts building, is a tiny hole-in-the-wall that makes the best crepes I have ever had, anywhere. I bought a feast's worth and went back up to the apartment, where I spent much of the day at the dining room table, working on the Conversation FSM.

Meanwhile, I was also trying to figure out what I could say that would convince John that we needed to have an FSM—and that it would go way more quickly if we brought back Gregory to work on it.

On the one hand, I was furious with the way that John and Milburn were mismanaging the project. On the other hand, the technology was exciting, and I was having fun, insofar as I was learning a lot about NLP. I was hoping I might eventually reduce Milburn's influence. If we could get to the point where John was the real CEO of the company, I was confident that I could convince him to run the project in a successful way. Whether I stayed with Celolot for the long-term really depended on whether we could get rid of Milburn. To that end, I hoped that once we got our prototype out the door, the sense of crisis would recede, and then Milburn could go back to his regular job and forget about us.

Monday, October 12th, 2015

After several rounds of email and conversations, I managed to convince John that we needed Gregory on our team, so John messaged Gregory and offered him another contract. This was to be open-ended but still part time. I was pleased to have Gregory working with us, though I was amazed that I had to fight so hard for so little. It should not have been a controversial decision.

Hwan was wrestling with a bug in his app that would log the user out without warning. The app wouldn't even tell the user that they were no longer logged in; it would simply become unresponsive. It was an intermittent bug, and it would take more than three weeks to fix.

Tuesday, October 13th, 2015

In the morning, I called Gregory to bring him up to speed on what I had done during the weekend. He caught on quickly, and then he took over. I was pleased to think that I could once again leave that work to him. I was able to refocus on getting the information out of Salesforce so we could feed it into the NLP app so that Sital could look up data that the user would expect us to know. Later, I worked with Sital to be sure he understood how to implement this in his code.

There was a strange silence from John. He did not respond to my emails nor my Slack messages. Since Sital was working at the incubator, I asked him if he'd seen John at all that day. Sital replied that John had been sitting right next to him all day, and was still there. That seemed creepy.

Around 10:00 P.M. John sent me a message on Slack.

John
The Board of Directors is frustrated with your lack of progress. Their consultant will call at 2 PM tomorrow. You will be required to explain why your software does not work.

Wednesday, October 14th, 2015

John told me that the consultant was an old friend of some of the board members, someone they trusted. He was described as a superstar of computer programming, a guy who had turned around many crippled teams, and he was going to come in to analyze my mistakes. He was going to save the situation.

This all made me feel like the company was planning to fire me. Even if I was inculpable, the consultant would lose nothing by blaming all current problems on me. Top tech consultants can charge in the range of $300 to $500 an hour, and with a bunch of investors desperate to save what they'd already spent, our project could transform this consultant's annual income from good to stellar.

I went over to the Twisted Branch Tea House and worked from there until it was time for the conference call. John and Hwan were already on by the time I connected. Then the consultant joined the call.

At first, John did all the talking, explaining the background and aims of the project. Then the consultant described himself. From the sounds of it, he had worked on some massive projects, big databases with hundreds of millions of users. Big beefy machines, big data center networking. Very impressive stuff. I had to respect him, even if he was being called in to replace me.

Then, the consultant asked what he was needed for. What was the problem?

John asked me to summarize the situation. I ticked through the big items: our initial plan was to do a complex but traditional app on the iPhone; Sital was a beginner and was unable to write a stable NLP app; then the board insisted on the Big Pivot; Hwan had to throw out his work and start over; we now faced the complexity of building an FSM that could manage our conversations; meanwhile Sital spent his days watching YouTube; therefore, Hwan and I had asked John to fire Sital.

John jumped in. He was embarrassed that I had mentioned Sital. He described what he felt was the real issue: small problems kept coming up on a day-to-day basis. The software needed to work, but it was just not working.

The conversation went on for another ten minutes, entirely between John and the consultant.

Finally, the consultant offered his conclusions:

- We were doing something that no one had ever tried before.
- Most NLP apps only handle "one response to one question"—like Siri on the iPhone—but we were going further; we were trying to track entire conversations over long periods of time.
- We were wrestling with personnel issues that needed to be addressed.
- We seemed to know what we were doing and simply needed time to get the work done.
- A project this ambitious was inevitably going to hit some tough moments. The board would have to accept that.
- He wouldn't be able to help. He would only slow us down.

John thanked him and promised to tell the board what had been said. We all hung up.

I was very pleased. That had gone much, much better than I had expected.

Then, John called me back, and he got Hwan to join the call. John was furious that I had mentioned Sital.

"You will not ever mention Sital!" shouted John.

"Every time!" I insisted. "Your choices regarding personnel are part of our story. We can't avoid talking about that if we expect a consultant to help us."

"Never again!" he shouted. "Do you hear me? You will never mention Sital again!"

"Every single time someone asks me why we are running late, I will mention your decision to stick with a novice employee when we clearly need an advanced expert!"

He was silent a moment, trying to think of a threat that would keep me from talking. "Well, listen, who we hire is part of our intellectual property and you are not allowed to reveal our intellectual property to outsiders!"

"If you honestly think that, then you have no idea what intellectual property is!" I shouted. Thankfully the Tea House was nearly empty at that hour.

I told John we could have finished the project a month sooner if we had had three excellent programmers. I told him he would have to take 100% of the blame for building a flawed team.

Then, his tone changed dramatically. Just like on July 28, as soon as the implication arose that he might be blamed for something, he retreated from anything that could sound like an accusation. Suddenly, he asserted there was no question of blame. Certainly, no one had ever blamed me for anything; the board was not blaming anyone for anything; this had merely been a fact-finding phone call to gather information.

I didn't want to let him worm his way out of this situation. Bringing up Slack on my screen, I read to him what he'd recently written to me:

"The board of directors is frustrated with your lack of progress."

"You are required to explain why your software does not work."

Were these not accusations?

Like a baby trying to avoid the next spoonful of carrot mush, he was dodgy. "You misread that message. They were simply looking for data. They were not blaming anyone for anything."

He and I went back and forth. The minutes dragged by, full of rage and avoidance. Finally, Hwan stepped in and played the diplomat. He suggested we focus on concrete tasks that would move the project forward. We spoke for another hour. Everyone calmed down.

Finally, John asked, "So, when the board asks me what is going on, should I just keep that information from you? Would that alleviate the pressure you feel?"

"John, you should be honest. I want you to share as much information as possible. But it would be nice if you sounded like you were on our side."

Hwan backed me up on this. He politely said to John, "You always sound like you are taking the side of the board. Lawrence is right—we'd like to feel that you're on our side."

I added, "If they ask why things are running late, it would be nice to think that you stand up for us and explain to the board that we are all working hard."

Then John insisted that there were no sides, that we were all on the same team, and that we should never feel there was an us-versus-them conflict between us and the board of directors.

All of which was a lie. Clearly there was a conflict between us and the board. And clearly John was on their side.

But at least for this one phone call, John promised he would do more to support us.

One suggestion that the consultant had was that we should all document our work. I was pleased to get his support on this issue. After the call, I sent an email to the entire team telling them that we had had a conversation with a very important consultant who was sent to us by the board, and the consultant said we should update our documentation. Only Gregory was religious about always keeping his documentation up to date.

THURSDAY, OCTOBER 15TH, 2015

I went to the Mudhouse coffee shop and worked all day on fetching data from Salesforce so I could feed it to the NLP library.

Hwan reached out to me and expressed his fear that the board of directors would cut off all of our funding. Should he be looking for another job?

At some point I got on the phone with John. I told him the current atmosphere of fear was counterproductive. Everyone was feeling the stress. John surprised me with a positive attitude that I had not heard since June.

There was no need for stress, he exclaimed! I should take vacation!

A vacation? At first I thought he was kidding, but he repeated himself several times: I should take a vacation. Something about the confrontation the day before had radically shifted his tone. He was swinging from extreme thrift to extreme generosity, the reverse of what he had done back on June 14. I was puzzled, but I decided to take him up on it; I would extend my trip into the next week, and treat the next Monday, Tuesday and Wednesday as actual days off.

The next day I took the commuter train to DC to work with Hwan directly. In the evening I returned to Charlottesville.

Monday, October 19th, 2015

John wrote to me:

> Awesom job rallying everyne last week nd making geat progress. You've done increddible and amazing work. Enjoy the time offf, and see you when you get back.

I was wary of this new tone, which was so positive and cheerful and supportive. I was pleased, since the intensity of the situation from September 17 to October 14 had been unsustainable, but I wasn't sure if this new tone was on a firm base, so I found myself expecting it to end whenever the next message arrived in my inbox.

Also, I had to wonder, did they think I was doing "increddible and amazing work" in the same way they thought that Sital was "a brilliantly creative data scientist of incredible genius"?

But this was a day when I supposed to be on vacation. I answered the questions I got in email and on Slack, but I quit early to go catch up with my Charlottesville friends.

Sunday, October 25th, 2015

I was back in New York, and some friends were visiting. I took them to the Museum of the City of New York, up on 103rd Street, so they could learn the history of the great metropolis. It's a fantastic place and probably deserves more attention than it gets.

Over the whole weekend, I didn't get a single work-related email, nor did I send any. There were no conversations on Slack. I don't believe that anyone did any work that weekend. The era of Hwan and I working very long hours was over. What was the point? The speed of the company would be determined by how slowly Sital went. If we weren't going to get rid of him, there was no point to excessive effort on the part of the rest of us.

Monday, October 26th, 2015

My first day back at the office after two weeks away.

Sital worked from home. John was meeting people again. Gregory wasn't working at all, because he had worked twenty hours over the weekend, and his contract restricted him to twenty-five hours a week.

The energy of the team was at a low ebb. It was as if we'd been told we had to run the hundred-meter dash, and when we reached the finish line we were told that we actually had to run two hundred meters, and when we finished that we were told it was a kilometer, then five, then ten. Eventually there comes a point when people realize they should have paced themselves, if only they had known what they were getting into. In early May it seemed clear that we would be done with Version 1.0 by August, but the board had changed the plans, so it was late October and we were only now nearing the finish line.

I wondered if John was also exhausted. But perhaps his feelings were not relevant: like an ox that was tired of pulling a plough, all that mattered was how badly its owner was willing to beat it.

Tuesday, October 27th, 2015

Toward 6:00 P.M. Milburn contacted John and scheduled a company meeting for 9:00 P.M., via video conference. Everyone was expected to attend.

At 9:00 P.M. John and I grabbed a conference room and set up a video connection. Although conference rooms were a scarce commodity during the day, at this hour only two of the four rooms were in use, so we had a choice about where to go. We picked the biggest room available. Hwan joined us via video from DC

Milburn's grim visage appeared before us on the screen. He launched straight into the accusations.

Why hadn't we developed any documentation about our project? he asked.

I pointed him to the wiki on GitHub.

Why hadn't we developed any documentation about our project? he asked again.

I was confused. Was he dismissing our documentation on GitHub?

"Do you know what a spec is?" he asked. That is, he was looking for a formal specification of the software we were suppose to write. Many books have been written on the subject, so I could have offered him a long answer, but I had the sense he wanted something pithy.

"A spec would be the documents that tell a group of engineers what they are building," I replied.

"So why haven't you written a spec?"

I couldn't understand why he was taking an accusatory tone. "We've written many documents that specify what should be built."

"You don't know what a spec is," he said.

"I don't know what a spec is?" I was surprised by this.

"You have no idea what a spec is."

"Should I send you the emails where I've detailed our architecture?"

"Oh, so you think an email is a spec?" he countered.

Here I stumbled into giving a sincere answer. "I think an email can serve as a rough draft for a spec, which can later be more formally specified on something like a wiki."

I later realized this kind of honesty was a mistake. None of his questions were sincerely meant, so I had exposed my innocence by answering sincerely.

"We are going to write a spec," he proclaimed. "A real one. Not a fake one."

Just then Hwan said, "I am terribly sorry, but I need to leave soon. I made commitments this evening before I knew we were meeting."

Milburn's reaction to this news bordered on uncouth. "Oh, you're leaving? You're leaving? Okay! Sure. What does it matter? Why not go? After all, who cares about this project? Why give a damn about this project?"

"I—I am very sorry," offered Hwan, who seemed almost ashamed of the fact that he had to leave.

"Sure, okay!" Milburn was almost spitting with anger. "Do you know how much Lawrence has been working? He's been working long hours."

I found it deeply suspicious that he would criticize me one moment, then praise me the next. Especially since Hwan had also been working long hours.

Milburn continued, "Go! Just go! I think it is clear where your real priorities are! Lawrence will be here working all night, while you get to have fun with your friends! Go have fun! Party all night!"

Hwan looked shocked that Milburn was making such a personal accusation. I was shocked too. I knew that Hwan had family obligations, and

113

assumed that's what was tearing him away, but whatever his reasons, they were his own private concern. (Much later I realized that Milburn had launched this attack in the hopes that Hwan would reveal exactly what his obligations were, as that would offer Milburn future ammunition.)

"Again, I am very sorry," said Hwan.

"Go!" shouted Milburn. "Just go! We don't want to hear your excuses! Just go! You obviously don't give a damn about this project! You never have! Lawrence has been working twenty hours a day to save this project, and you just don't give a damn!"

"I am very, very sorry," Hwan whispered.

John was grinning, almost laughing. I had the feeling he'd seen this routine from Milburn many times before.

"We'll talk to you tomorrow," said John, half-laughing, and he switched off Hwan's video feed.

Milburn had boasted that I worked twenty hours a day, but he wasn't offering a real compliment; he was just using me as a convenient weapon with which he could bash Hwan. I was slow to realize what kind of conversation I was in, the fundamental manipulation at the heart of it. Confused, I wondered why, if John had told Milburn that I was working long hours, he had failed to mention that Hwan was also working long hours.

Cursed by an assumption of goodwill, I very nearly opened my mouth to correct Milburn's misimpression of Hwan. Thankfully my brain began to catch up with the situation. If Milburn was willing to ignore the facts, or twist them to suit his current needs, then my defending Hwan would have simply revealed how little I understood what Milburn was attempting to do.

After all, was Milburn really angry, or was it faux outrage? Did Milburn seriously think he could announce a meeting at 6:00 P.M. and expect everyone to shift their plans so that they were free at 9:00 P.M.? Perhaps this meeting was simply a test, to see how loyal we were. Why call a late meeting on such short notice, other than to see who was willing to cancel all of their other plans?

Milburn was supposed to be a fantastic salesperson. He always exceeded his monthly quotas. But the only people who are great at sales are those who are great at manipulating others.

We ended on an ominous note. Milburn asserted that the project had been badly managed, but he did not offer details. He certainly wasn't apologizing for his own series of miscalculations regarding the Big Pivot, nor was he saying that John had been a disaster as a manager. He was saying the project had been badly managed because of something the programmers had done. Then he declared we would talk more the following day.

Wednesday, October 28th, 2015

At 11:00 A.M., John and Sital and I went into a conference room and set up a video call with Milburn. Hwan joined us via video again. After a moment, Milburn's extremely overweight torso and face appeared on screen.

Milburn was smiling. He spoke with a gentle voice.

"How about that game last night?" he opened with.

Milburn was in a good mood? Interesting, okay. Cool. Sital and John both watched sports.

Everyone started to discuss the epic battle between the Royals and the Mets in the first game of the World Series. The game had lasted fourteen innings, tying for the longest game in the history of the World Series! Alcides Escobar hit the first World Series inside-the-park home run since the World Series of 1929! Stuff like this almost never happens in baseball!

In that moment Milburn wanted to convince us that he was our friend, our buddy, our chum—someone we could hang out with and have a beer with and joke about the referees making bad calls. Sital made a remark about how suddenly the game had turned around at some point; John laughed, and Milburn laughed, and they were all good fellows sharing a laugh.

Arguably, this was part of what had allowed Milburn to become so successful. First he creates a friendly feeling, then he gets angry and he makes his new friends feel guilty for letting him down.

It did not take long before the laughing ended and the anger started.

"So where is the spec?" inquired Milburn.

He insisted that we could not make any progress until we had a written spec. I again directed him to the documentation on GitHub, which he again dismissed without giving a reason.

We then spent four hours writing down what Milburn referred to as "the spec." This was mostly an exercise so that he could gain an understanding of the software. We walked him through the various scenarios: what happens when a user first logs in, what happens when login credentials expire, what happens when a user forgets to send us a mandatory field. He apparently felt this was important work, but I mourned the loss of a day spent in a meeting. In particular, I mourned the loss of momentum. We were very close to being done, and it seemed stupid to throw a day away. If Milburn wanted to help, he could have joined us back in May.

Much later, it occurred to me that he knew we were almost done, and that was precisely why he decided to join us now: so that he could take credit for the final success. If the Big Pivot had destroyed his credibility with the rest of the board of directors, then being able to take credit for our working software now would restore their faith in him. If that was his plan, it was a clever move.

We ended up with a high-level document that was too much of a summary to offer any benefit to us as programmers, but it was absolutely the kind of summary I would have written for the board of directors.

Toward evening, Gregory joined us via video. He was adding the final confirmation step to his Conversation FSM. In other words, after we had collected all the data, the user would need to either confirm or indicate that they wished to edit.

So what text should we look for? Many of the possibilities are obvious: "yes," "confirm," "ok," etc., but what about possible slang? "Sure"? "Awesome"? "Luvit"? How many affirmative words should we program for? What about a smiling emoji?

Long ago the tech industry adopted the term "bikeshedding" from C. Northcote Parkinson's 1957 book, *Parkinson's Law* to describe why some issues generate intense discussion not because they are important, but because everyone can understand them.

Consider what happens at a typical office when a difficult technical issue is discussed. Perhaps there is the question of whether the company should use SQL or NoSQL databases. If the top management is non-technical, they will simply ask their engineers to generate a report, and then they will follow whatever advice the engineers recommend.

Now imagine, instead, the question is, "What color should we paint the office?" This is a question that everyone can understand, so everyone has an opinion.

Some people will want warm, bright colors: "We should paint the office orange and red because those colors are vibrant and give me a positive outlook!"

Some people hate bright colors: "Are you out of your mind? This is an *office*, not a school nursery! I refuse to work at a place that looks like some four-year-old's idea of a good Mother's Day card!"

Some people love cooler colors: "Blue is calm, dignified. It puts people in the mood to do serious work, it suggests gravitas and importance."

Some people hate cooler colors: "Blue is so depressing! Blue makes me want to slit my wrists! I'd need to triple my dose of Lexapro if we paint this office blue!"

That's bikeshedding. Unimportant issues get way more discussion than important issues, simply because people have a better understanding of the unimportant issues.

We were now engaged in an hour of the most severe bikeshedding that I can remember. Milburn, a member of the board of directors, was actively involved in a conversation with us about how many slang terms we should watch for when users confirm their data.

The level of micro-management was ridiculous. But even more asinine was the fact that we were ignoring important issues so we could discuss an unimportant issue that Milburn understood.

Only one good thing came out of that meeting. I pointed out that we had not had Hwan up to New York since June, and we would be able to wrap up the final work more effectively if he came and worked with us. John agreed that on Monday we would bring Hwan up to New York.

Gregory and I were in agreement about the most important issue that we still needed to resolve. Let's say a user had all the data filled in and we expected them to confirm it, but instead they indicated they wanted to engage in further edits. How did we get that request back to the iPhone? We worked until midnight, when Gregory had to go.

At 12:15 A.M. Varak and Perrino began playing *League of Legends*, and I stood behind them and watched as they annihilated team after team. They were very good. We ordered pizza and drank beer, and then very late, we traded stories about odd people we had worked with at various companies. Here was, no doubt, a competition that I could win. I had definitely worked with some odd people.

Thursday, October 29th, 2015

I woke at 9:00 A.M., made breakfast, and took a shower. It was almost 11:00 A.M. when I headed out the door. Milburn called me and asked where I was. I explained that, at this point in the project, I mostly had to work with Gregory, and Gregory only worked evenings. I reminded Milburn that Gregory should be full time with us but that we had not hired him fast enough, so now we only got him at night.

Milburn snapped, "I understand how disappointed you must be that you are unable to do the job we hired you for." Then he hung up.

I now had a member of the board of directors calling me on my personal cell phone and asking me where I was. This level of pressure was not healthy. Either Milburn would soon go away and leave us alone, or would find other work.

At 5:00 P.M. we all had another video conference with Milburn. I was told it would last fifteen minutes, and we would only need to explain what

117

we had accomplished that day. Instead, it lasted ninety minutes, and we got dragged back into the debate over which words a user could use to indicate that they wanted to confirm their data. What about "Excellent" and "Go" and even "K"? Milburn felt we should add all of those in.

I was trying to test the whole system but something had broken. Everyone had submitted new code that day, so I was not sure whose new code was to blame. Everything seemed to indicate another bug in Sital's code. Before I quit for the night I sent an email to the team, saying:

The bug seems to be in the Transform class that Sital wrote, but I am not sure which function.

Milburn quickly responded via email:

I would like to again ask that we not call out individuals, but the apps.

Sital had left for the day, but John was still there, so I turned to him and asked, "Hey, what is this? Am I not allowed to honestly report what I find and whose code is to blame?"

John said, "Look, I get that Sital has caused a lot of problems, but he is our NLP expert."

"And why is that?" I asked. "In early September you promised we would fire him within three weeks. That was six weeks ago. Why haven't you fired him yet?"

"We need to raise some money first."

"Well, when are you getting this money?"

"I don't know, but we need him on the team until we do. We will absolutely fire him when we get more money, but till then, he stays with us."

"Why is that?" I asked again.

"Because we can't raise money unless we have an NLP expert," he declared.

"The great majority of all the bugs we've had to deal with have been in his code. You *know* how much he has slowed us down. We could have been done a month ago if we were working with someone competent."

Exasperated, he shouted, "I know, but we've got to keep him on the team till we have enough money to hire someone better!"

That night I found the bug, and sure enough, it was in some code that Sital had written. I sent a message to the team documenting the problem, and just to rile up Milburn I made sure to include the words, "This was in the code written by Sital."

Later the whole team got an email in reply:

Lawrence, I am deeply grateful to you for tracking down the source of this problem. You have been a great help to us, and you've been a wonderful support for Sital. He is a brilliantly creative data scientist of incredible genius, but we are at such an early stage, we have not been able to take full advantage of his astonishing skills. Clearly, the menial tasks that we have given him are not his strength, which is why we have you on staff. As we venture deeper into the complex depths of Artificial Intelligence and Machine Learning, Sital's awesome abilities will be ever more crucial to us, but at this time we depend on you to be sure that the simple stuff works.

This email came from John's account, but the psychological manipulation fit Milburn's pattern.

For weeks now, John had been verbally willing to admit that Sital was a source of problems. But in Slack or in email, anything that could later be shown in a court of law, Sital was always flawless. And why would they cover for him so much? Were they getting money from naive investors by telling them that we had on our team "a brilliantly creative data scientist of incredible genius"? And how many times could they possibly use that exact, repetitive, worn-out phrase? It had become ludicrous.

Friday, October 30th, 2015

We had a video conference with Milburn at noon. He said he wanted a fifteen-minute "agile scrum session," but it stretched to forty minutes.

Milburn started off by telling us that we needed project management software. He glared at us. Why hadn't we thought of this?

Everyone had an opinion about this topic. John stated that we did have project management software (PivotalTracker), but some developers (he meant me) didn't update their tasks. I replied that we were misusing PivotalTracker by marking tasks as "done" when they were not done. Sital wanted to use Jira; Hwan wanted to find software that was lightweight.

I argued that the best project management software in the world wouldn't help us if we didn't have a good project manager in charge, and conversely, if we had a good project manager, then it wouldn't matter if they preferred to write their notes on crumpled-up napkins.

The crucial issue was who had the power to reject work. That is, who had the power to say, "Hey, this isn't done yet." We'd fought about this all summer; John and Sital would mark a task "done" when it still had bugs.

John was a terrible project manager because he got bored. Testing can be tedious. A good project manager has to have the patience to test the same thing ten times. Sometimes twenty times. Sometimes fifty times.

Milburn declared that from now on we were *all* responsible for project management. I thought this was a frustrating dodge. He wanted to reserve for himself the power to say whether something was done, but he did not want to get dragged into the tedious task of testing something ten or twenty or fifty times. Effectively, this meant we would have no project manager. Without a project manager, the discussion over project management software struck me as utterly futile.

Then we started talking about what needed to happen next. Milburn wanted to know the exact problem we were facing at that moment. I gave a high-level overview and then he demanded more detail. Back in the 1990s, Milburn had been an early user of Microsoft Excel and eventually became very good at it. He even learned how to program in Visual Basic, so he considered himself something of a computer programmer.

If he engaged in the conversation as someone who was moderately technical, I would have been comfortable with the fact that he understood programming more than most non-technical people. But he instead insisted that we think of him as someone with advanced skills. Was he aware that his programming experience was limited and completely out of date? He gave no indication.

Hwan suggested that we should test the whole system together as much as possible; we should not test the pieces in isolation.

Milburn became obsessed with this idea. It's so obvious! Why are we testing our code in isolation? Are we idiots? Why not test the whole system together?

I pointed out that testing the whole system together would mean pulling all of the apps together on a central server and testing them using the app from the iPhone. Milburn looked at me like I was an imbecile. Obviously we should do what I just said, why would we not want to do that?

He pursed his lips and knitted his fingers together. "Once you have your code on the same server, you can all test the same code. Instead of testing stuff on your local machines, where you never know if your stuff matches up with anyone else's stuff, just push it all to a central server and then you know whether or not your stuff works together."

I explained that when I test code on my machine, I can see a bug, fix it, recompile, and re-test, all in a minute or less. If I have to test on a central server, I need to push all my code to the central server and recompile there—and then my find-fix-recompile-retest cycle is about eight minutes long instead of one minute long, so I end up fixing seven or eight lines of code per hour instead of sixty.

Milburn became sarcastic. "The difference between my system and your system is that my system takes eight minutes and yours takes two months! If you had just tested the whole system together then you would have been done in August!"

Hwan felt that Milburn had misunderstood the situation, so he spoke at some length about the advantage of using an iPhone emulator to test the whole system locally. These were good ideas.

Milburn loved what Hwan was saying. "Use an emulator! Test everything locally that way! It's easy! All your problems thus far are because you haven't done enough testing. You've got to run it on your machines and see that everything really works!"

I pointed out, "You just said the exact opposite thing two minutes ago. You said you wanted us to push everything to a central server."

Milburn sat back in his chair and adopted an injured tone, "Oh, okay, Lawrence, I see. I'm the bad guy, and you're the good guy. Everything I say is stupid, and everything you say is smart. I'm a complete bozo, and you're a genius. That's why we're two months late, right?"

Nobody spoke. Milburn stared at me through the screen. I could not decide what the best response was, so I kept a poker face. Perhaps he was expecting me to apologize? A surprisingly long moment passed during which no one moved.

Since John loathed conflict, he had a tendency to end any uncomfortable silence. So at that moment he piped up that we should all try to do more testing. And of course, that is a generic statement, like saying parents should love their children, so who's going to argue? Testing is good. The only disagreement we'd had was over what kind of testing.

Gregory suggested it might be more productive if we all got to work. Milburn agreed, but he insisted that we work while we were logged into a video chat with him. Wait, seriously? We glanced at each other, wondering if he was really going to carry out this demand. Sure enough, he mandated that we go to our desks and work while logged into a video chat. And Milburn just sort of stared at us through the screen, all those haunting little pixels fixated on our every move. He wanted to scrutinize us. He wanted to overhear us. His attitude was like that of a sheriff's foreman who was overseeing a convict crew made to dig a ditch. It was as if he feared that we would only work while he was looking at us, and the moment he looked away, we would goof off.

Gregory had already offered to team up with me to investigate the most important bug we were facing, which was somewhere inside the NLP-converter app, possibly inside of Sital's code. And Milburn was listening.

I had recently given Gregory full responsibility for the NLP-converter app; in situations like this, however, I would work on it anyway, since I still understood it better than Gregory.

Gregory offered his opinion. "On line 239 I don't think we have the 'user_id' set yet."

I said, "It's definitely in the hashmap."

Milburn jumped in. "What is this? Hashmaps? Shouldn't you be sending JSON documents?"

He had absolutely no idea what he was talking about.

I replied, trying to keep my composure, "Milburn, JSON is the serialization format we use when our apps send messages to each other. But now we are inside of an app, and we use hashmaps."

Milburn went quiet for a moment, but he was still watching.

Then Gregory brought up what he felt was the real issue. "Hey, I don't see where we initialize our NLP engine. Are you sure you set this up so it's initialized?"

Milburn asked eagerly, "Gregory? Are you saying Lawrence forgot to turn the software on? That's incredible."

Gregory tried to correct him. "No, no, I'm just asking where is this initialized ..."

I said calmly, "Gregory, look in 'core.clj' and you'll see the start function."

Milburn was still in love with the idea that I had made a serious mistake, so he tried to get Gregory to pursue it further. "But, Gregory, do you see where Lawrence initialized the NLP engine?"

Gregory said, "No, I don't see that."

Milburn was delighted. He leaned forward, toward the screen. "So Lawrence forgot to set up the code correctly?"

I spoke again directly to Gregory, trying to pretend as though Milburn didn't exist. "Gregory, you have to look in the 'start.clj' file."

Gregory looked, but he still asked, "Are you sure this is being called?"

Yes, I was sure, but I had never had my credibility attacked the way Milburn was attacking mine, so I figured I should document everything. "I can check on the server."

And Milburn, instead of waiting till I had checked, started fuming. "I can't believe this. I can't believe this. This is absolutely incredible."

I logged in to the staging server and ran a search on the logs, looking for the special startup message that I had coded. I saw that it appeared six times that day, which made sense, because I had made six changes to the app and I'd restarted it six times.

I explained straightforwardly, "Sure, if I run 'grep' on the logs I see the startup message six times."

That should have killed that whole conversation. But Milburn would not let go of the idea that I had made some terrible mistake, so he kept prodding, "But, Gregory, do you actually see the line of code that initiates the NLP engine?"

Gregory found the line and then Milburn asked him to pursue it further: was it possible that Lawrence had screwed up something inside of the initiation process? Those two went off on a tangent that lasted over an hour. It was a good experience for Gregory, I think, because it forced him to walk through all of my code and really learn it. But in terms of fixing the bug we were supposed to be fixing, it was an incredible waste of time.

As it turned out, there was no one particular bug that was stopping the system. There were dozens of small bugs, all over the place, and the only way to fix them was by patiently stepping through the code, finding them, and fixing them one at a time. There were bugs in the code that Gregory wrote, there were bugs in the code that Sital wrote, and there were bugs in the code that I wrote. All of that was to be expected, given the phase of development we were at.

After about two more hours of this, Milburn began to rant about how we had taken a very simple problem and turned it into a big complicated thing. I did not challenge him this time, but I was fascinated that he and John had both been entirely unwilling to recognize how ambitious this project was. Even Apple, with all of its money and engineers, had never attempted anything as ambitious as what we were now trying to do. With Celolot's product, a salesperson would be engaging in a conversation which would have an unlimited number of interactions, and the result needed to be cumulative over an indeterminate amount of time.

For example, a salesperson might write, "Create a new record of sale. I just sold $1 million of cleaning supplies to Hilton Hotels."

Then our software would write back, "Please confirm, the client is Hilton Hotels, the amount is $1,000,000, and the product is cleaning supplies."

And then the salesperson might write: "That's correct."

And then the software would write: "What is the start date for this contract?"

And then the salesperson might write: "I don't know yet."

Then we would check to see if we can create this record of sale, and we would have to deal with what circumstances come up—for instance, we might find that we cannot create the record of sale because the salesperson works for a company that insists that the "start_date" field is mandatory.

So then our software says: "Your company has decided that the 'start_date' is mandatory, so we cannot create a record of sale at this time."

And the salesperson says: "Okay, just keep this in memory and I'll get back to you with the start date."

The next day the salesperson calls Hilton Hotels and they work out the start date for the contract, and the salesperson writes to the app: "For Hilton Hotels, the start date is November 1st."

And then we find the conversation from yesterday, and we give it the start date, and then we can create the record of sale in Salesforce.

That is a lot more complicated than Siri. We were tracking the whole accumulated meaning of a conversation over the course of days.

Eventually, Milburn stopped lecturing us about how simple the project

123

was, and gradually he got bored of watching us. Unless you are a computer programmer, it is not exciting to watch a computer programmer work. (In fact, even if you *are* a computer programmer, watching another programmer fix bugs, one line at a time, is rarely exciting.)

But Milburn engaged in one final trick. He turned off his video feed, yet he left his computer logged in to the chat room. Now we could not see whether he was there.

Some hours later I found a bug in Sital's code, and I asked if Milburn was there. "Milburn? Milburn, are you there? Milburn?"

No answer. So at some point he had snuck away, but he had wanted us to think that he was still there, watching us.

Typically, I enjoy pair programming. I enjoy talking through problems with other programmers. But writing code while Milburn listened was like pair programming with Genghis Khan.

As much as I loved the project we were working on, it occurred to me that this was becoming a hostile environment. I decided that Milburn would either stop bothering us, or I would have to quit.

Around 9:00 P.M. a wizard came into the incubator … then a barbarian with a fake axe made of cardboard … then Wonder Woman, accompanied by a sexy nurse. It was the night before Halloween, and the incubator was even weirder than usual. They harassed Varak until he finally gave up working and left with them. I decided to head out, too, while the night was still young.

Sunday, November 1st, 2015

I decided it was crucial to reassure the team that we were on schedule and that everything was going to be okay, so long as we stayed focused and maintained discipline with regard to what each of our apps needed from each of the other apps (that is, I wanted them to keep the Github wiki up to date).

I wrote two emails. In the first email, I reminded everyone of the importance of documentation. In the second email, I copied and pasted portions of two earlier emails, from August 31st and September 3rd. In these excerpts, I had offered a realistic estimate suggesting that the initial system would be stable once we had a fully functional Conversation FSM—which I had suggested would take four weeks of full-time work or eight weeks of part-time work. Now it was early November and we were almost done, so my estimate was on track to come true. I also offered an estimate of when the app would be complete: roughly six more months of work to implement all the features on our wish list, so we should be done in the spring of 2016.

The previous week was a disaster for our productivity. I was furious about the time we had lost catering to Milburn's various requests. Although I still loved the technology we were building, we'd now veered deep into the territory of dysfunctional mismanagement. Back in Virginia I'd spent six years working with a business partner whose erratic swings had lost us many opportunities. I was unwilling to invest any more of my life on projects that seemed unlikely to succeed. For the sake of the project, Milburn needed to go back to his regular job and leave us alone. If the previous week was a fluke, then I'd be excited to get back to work in the morning, but if Milburn continued to interfere then I would need to quit.

MONDAY, NOVEMBER 2ND, 2015

I woke up and got ready for work. Still at my apartment, I checked my work email. I saw that Milburn had sent me a short email:

Why did you send those emails over the weekend? Please call me as soon as you get to the office.

I was surprised. Did he really want to start the week with another argument? And why did he have to take issue with those emails, when they were the epitome of common sense?

In an attempt to give him one last chance to think about what he was doing, I replied:

I send email all the time. Do we now have a policy that says I cannot communicate with my coworkers? That is unusual.

I went to the office. I settled in and checked GitHub, and I pulled all the latest code that anyone had committed. A few minutes later, Hwar showed up. I was excited to see him. I had not seen him since October 16, and he had not been to New York since June. We started to talk about what we should accomplish while he was in New York.

125

Then John came over. He was on the phone with Milburn. I heard John say, "Yes, he's here. I'll tell him to call you."

I found a private corner of the incubator and gave Milburn a call.

"Good morning, Milburn. What can I do for you?"

He skipped salutations altogether: "I asked you to call me. Why didn't you call me?" He sounded sad and angry simultaneously.

"I just got to work, and Hwan got here from DC. We simply stopped for a chat."

"I asked you to call me. It's a simple request. Just a phone call."

A long pause.

"Yes, sir, but I just got to work, and Hwan got here at the same time."

"It's a simple request! Basic politeness. I wrote you an email, I made a request, and you ignored the request. I had to call John, and John had to pressure you to pick up the phone."

"I was aware that we would be speaking soon. We have a conference call coming up, don't we?"

"I made a very simple request, and you deliberately decided to ignore it. Basic human decency should have been enough for you to honor that request, but I guess you don't believe in basic human decency. And you decided not to call."

He paused. I said nothing. After a long silence, he continued:

"You decided not to call. That is not nice. It's rude, it's disrespectful, and I'm hurt. As a human being, as someone with feelings, I am hurt, and I would like an apology."

He sounded like he was going to cry. The note of self-pity surprised me.

My friends and I have sometimes discussed the right-wing television personality Glenn Beck and his tendency to cry on television. Is Beck truly overwhelmed with emotion as frequently as it seems, or is it all just an act? The best explanation I had ever heard, from a friend of mine who is a professional actress, was that a great actor fully experiences the emotions they're portraying—so it's possible that Beck is both playing a character and also genuinely feeling his emotional raptures. I think something similar must be true of Milburn. On the one hand, it seems naive to think that he really felt such strong emotions over my failure to call him, but on the other hand, his emoting seemed entirely sincere.

"I received an email from you stating that you would like to talk, but we have a meeting scheduled at one and—"

"I told you to call me!"

"—I knew we were going to talk."

"I told you to *call* me! Don't send a bullshit email! Pick up the phone if I tell you to pick up the phone!"

The innocent often believe that salespeople aim to be nice all the time, but this is based on encounters with retail-level salespeople who have to work with customers who they don't know. And when the type of retail is known for narrow profits, then the salespeople don't have time to get to know the customers—because the game is all about volume, not closing a few big deals.

But if a product has fat profits, or the industry *is* all about a few big deals, then the best salespeople get to know their customers and use all personal information as a weapon. If you go to buy lipstick, the salespeople will often be nice, because they don't have much leverage over you. But if you go back to the same store repeatedly, a good salesperson will learn your weaknesses. Maybe you are worried about your thinning hair. Maybe you are worried about your weight. Maybe you have lines around your eyes. Every weakness is a potential sale.

If the obvious forms of manipulation fail to work, then a great salesperson will get nasty. Okay, reject their advice, don't take care of yourself. That's fine. Let yourself go, look like a wreck. Why care that your children will be embarrassed when their friends see you? Why care that your husband will lust after other women? You'll be a terrible mother and partner, but hey, I guess it's okay to be selfish, right?

Every industry has certain euphemisms for the least savory aspects of its business. In sales, there is the secretly ugly phrase, "goal-oriented." That sounds pleasant, doesn't it? If I point at a woman and I say, "That entrepreneur is goal-oriented," then you probably think I am complimenting her. But if I point at her and say, "That entrepreneur is a lying, manipulative, soulless psychopath who brutally exploits labor from the eleven-year-olds she employs in her sweatshops in Indonesia," then you probably think I am insulting her, unless you are a libertarian. And yet both statements mean about the same thing: that she is someone who is willing to do whatever is necessary to ensure the success of her business.

When I read about Milburn online, I'd seen testimonials from his colleagues in which he was often described as a goal-oriented salesperson. That probably meant that he was a master of manipulating other people's emotions. He knew all the tricks: praise, shame, laughter, anger, promises, guilt, threats.

Whether his use of these tools was conscious or unconscious is, of course. But it doesn't matter much. A lifetime as a sales professional left him with an arsenal of psychological ploys that had become second nature to him.

In this current situation, he surely knew that once a person apologizes, the apology sets a precedent for the conversation, and the person who apologizes tends to continue to apologize. But that much is Psychology 101, and I was aware of the trap. For this reason, I avoided apologizing.

"I was confused by the email that you sent. It sounded like you wanted to talk about the fact that I sent emails to my—"

"You are wasting the time of your coworkers, when they are trying to stay focused on getting the next release out. Does that interest you at all? Do you want us to get the next release out?"

Shame and guilt. There he was, skillfully wielding those tools from his sales-tactics tool belt.

"Milburn, I have been working very long hours to try to get the next release out."

"The time you spent writing those emails is time you could have spent debugging your software. But I guess that doesn't interest you, does it?"

Effectively, he was saying that I was no longer allowed to communicate with my coworkers regarding any issue except for a small set of issues that he would arbitrarily define. That wouldn't make sense if he wanted me to maximize my effectiveness as an experienced programmer, but it would make a lot of sense if he simply wanted me to stop putting so many of my opinions into written form. Assuming it was his idea, and his alone, to use our "brilliantly creative data scientist of incredible genius" as a trap for unwary investors, then my emails would be quite a revelation to the rest of the board of directors and to any disgruntled investors.

A line such as, "But I guess that doesn't interest you, does it?" is never meant in a literal sense; it is always thrown out there to show that the speaker has the power to throw it out there. The previous Tuesday he had praised me for working long hours and shamed Hwan for not working as late as I did, yet now he wanted to suggest that I was lazy and didn't want to work.

"Who am I to you, right now?"

"You are Milburn Jennings, a member of the Celolot Board of Directors."

"Yes, that's right, but who else am I?"

For the life of me, I could not imagine what he wanted me to say. Did he want to hear something stupid like, "We are teammates!" or "You are my friend!"? At a stretch, I could imagine he wanted to hear something like, "You are an investor in Celolot," but I did not actually know if he was an investor or just a board member, so I couldn't say that.

"Who else are you?"

"Yes, who am I to you?"

"Uh, I'm not sure what you are looking for."

"I AM THE LEADER OF THE TECH TEAM!"

I was unable to hide my surprise. "Oh?"

"And do you know why I am the leader of the tech team?"

I said nothing.

"Do you know why I am the leader of the tech team?"

Again I said nothing.

"BECAUSE YOU FAILED!"

In court, lawyers typically follow the rule, "Do not ask any question unless you already know the answer." I knew to adopt that rule in an adversarial situation such as this. That meant censoring the first few responses that came into my head. I wanted to ask, "How do you define failure?" but that would have been like handing him a sledgehammer and inviting him to take his best shot.

I filtered out any questions and instead stuck to firm counter-assertions.

"This project is on time."

"You could've done something great. You could've come in here and been a real leader. You could've shown the world what you were made of. But you decided to do nothing. You decided you'd rather sit around and complain. You didn't lead this team. You don't know how to lead. Admit it. I want to hear you say it. Admit that you failed."

"We have built some very impressive technology. This is a service that has to deal—"

"ARE YOU MAN ENOUGH TO ADMIT YOU FAILED?"

"—with massively concurrent real-world communications going between multiple points, from the iPhone to our servers, though our NLP—"

"ARE YOU MAN ENOUGH TO ADMIT YOU FAILED?"

"—engine, sometimes back to the iPhone and other times to Salesforce. And we have built a working demo—"

"ARE YOU MAN ENOUGH TO ADMIT YOU FAILED?"

"—in a remarkably short amount of time."

He was silent for a moment after I finished. I looked around the incubator and watched all the other people, at all the other startups, working hard on their projects. I wasn't sure what Milburn was waiting for. I wasn't sure what he expected me to say.

I took out my iPhone and I started texting Natalie. I sent her bits of what Milburn had said to me.

A very long moment passed in silence. He was waiting for me to speak, and I was waiting for him to speak. Actually, I was waiting for him to hang up so I could go and get some actual work done.

"You can't do it, can you?" he finally asked.

I stayed silent.

"You can't do it, can you?"

I stayed silent some more.

"You can't admit that you failed. Because that hurts, and you don't like to feel hurt, do you?"

This was a guy who was almost crying a few minutes ago because I didn' give him a phone call. It was quite an accusation for him to now throw at me

Another very long silence followed. He was hoping that I would tall into the silence. That's the kind of mistake that John always made. I also used to make that mistake; I suppose we all do when we are young. It's an easy trick whereby those who are good at verbal combat can get thei opponent to sabotage themselves: create an awkward silence and then se if the other person feels compelled to say something.

He let out a long sigh.

"So where are we right now? Where is the software? What more need to happen?"

"We are stuck at the point where we call the NLP 'model' that Sital ha built, so I assume there is some problem in Sital's code."

A long silence passed.

"You like to blame others, don't you? Does that make you feel good, when you blame other people? I've heard you blame Sital, I've heard you blame Hwan, I've heard you blame Gregory, but you know who you never blame? You never blame yourself. I've never heard you say one bad thing about yourself. And yet every single time you blame Sital or Hwan or Gregory, in the end, when we find the real problem, it always turns out to be you. All of our problems go back to you, but you never take responsibility for what you've done."

Several things occurred to me at once:

First, I could repeat these words, verbatim, about Milburn himself, and the statement would be true. Certainly, if the board of directors felt we were running late, the root problem was Milburn's decision to proceed with the Big Pivot back in July.

Second, it would be a mistake to treat any of what he said as rational.

Third, the only accusation I'd ever thrown at Hwan or Gregory was that they were relentlessly talented. Their excellence was noteworthy. My serious criticisms had been confined to Sital's programming and John's managing.

Fourth, it would be a mistake to respond as if we were having a good faith conversation, eagerly trying to discover the real facts of the situation or discussing the interesting ideas that could make Cielolot better. The conversation had become a pure power struggle.

"We have added debugging statements to every function in the system," I tried to explain, "and the code runs until we call Sital's model. That strongly indicates that there is a problem in that model."

"Why didn't you foresee this problem and put in some guards against it?"

"We have made huge progress making this code more and more stable. We are on track to meet our deadline this week."

"Can you guarantee that the project will be complete on Friday? Every bug is fixed? We can put this in the hands of a customer on Friday, and you guarantee it?"

"I don't want to speak to—"

"IT'S A YES OR NO QUESTION!"

"—how much Hwan or Sital still need to do, or how—"

"IT'S A YES OR NO QUESTION!"

"—many hours Gregory feels he can work this week."

"IT'S A YES OR NO QUESTION!"

"It is not a yes or no question!"

"IT'S A YES OR NO QUESTION!"

"It is not a yes or no question!"

"WILL YOU MAN UP AND GIVE ME A YES OR NO ANSWER FOR ONCE?!"

130

"It is *not* a yes or no question! I cannot take responsibility for Hwan or Sital or Gregory!"

"THAT'S RIGHT! YOU CAN'T TAKE RESPONSIBILITY FOR ANYTHING!"

"Why have more than one programmer if I can write all the code myself? Why did you even hire Hwan or Gregory or Sital if you thought I could get this project done by myself?"

"IF YOU ARE LEAD OF THE TECH TEAM THEN YOU TAKE RESPONSIBILITY FOR THE TECH TEAM!"

"If I am the lead developer at Celolot, then why are we ignoring the estimate I gave in August?"

"Oh, I see. I get it. You don't want to be lead developer any more, is that it? Too much responsibility? Is that it? When the going gets tough, Lawrence goes home. Is that it? Well, I just looked at your LinkedIn profile. Do you know what it says there? IT SAYS YOU ARE LEAD DEVELOPER AT CELOLOT!"

"What about John's responsibilities? If I am the lead developer, then—"

"IT SAYS YOU ARE LEAD DEVELOPER AT CELOLOT!"

"—why can't I get rid of Sital and why can't I get someone better—"

"IT SAYS YOU ARE LEAD DEVELOPER AT CELOLOT!"

"—as a replacement? And why can't I get Gregory hired full-time?"

"ONCE YOU RING THAT BELL YOU CAN'T UNRING IT! IT SAYS YOU ARE LEAD DEVELOPER AT CELOLOT!"

I wasn't even sure what that meant, and it's possible that Milburn didn't know either. Milburn was very, very good at this kind of verbal combat, and he had clearly learned long ago that he could win a fight like this by getting the advantage and keeping it. And a person doesn't need to make sense in order to keep the advantage; sometimes it's enough to simply shout loudly until the other person backs down.

To the extent that he had any kind of rational point, he seemed to imply that, because I was the most experienced person on the tech team, I should take on the responsibilities of being CTO. But for the first four months I'd been at Celolot, I was told that Dennis was the CTO. I also recalled that when John had encouraged the rest of the team to pick titles, he said we could pick any title for ourselves *besides* CTO. If they had wanted me to be CTO, then they would have needed to pay me more, and I would have demanded complete honesty and direct access to the board of directors.

Much later, I thought about what he had said: "I just went and looked at your LinkedIn page …" That is a truly revealing remark. Before I had called him, he knew he was going to need some ammunition to use against me, so he had checked out my LinkedIn page in the hopes of finding something. He had probably also checked out my blog and my other online sites. That says a lot about how he operates. Although he seems to engage in sudden bouts of rage, he actually plans his attacks carefully, just as any good salesperson carefully plans each sales call. His actions are probably deliberate, even though he tries to create the illusion that his emotions are spontaneous.

And of course, we never talked about the idea that the CEO should take responsibility for anything. Was there, at this moment, an unspoken awareness that John was Milburn's assistant, and John had been given the title of CEO just for fun, because Milburn did not need another credential on his resume? In a startup with just three programmers and one CEO, four people in total, the CEO would normally take some responsibility for the progress of the tech team.

"No one ever told you September," Milburn barked.

"Pardon?"

"No one ever told you September."

"I'm ... I'm honestly not sure what you mean," I replied.

"In your bullshit email," Milburn retorted. "'Stable and feature complete.' No one ever told you September. No one ever said that to you."

For the life of me, I could not imagine what he meant. "September?"

"Don't you parse my words! Don't you dare do that! Don't try to derail this conversation again!

Milburn truly had a genius for the strategic use of anger. If he sensed the risk of losing control of the conversation, he would indulge in another outburst. If I were to ever switch over to the Dark Side, I would want to study with him. His techniques were fundamentally dishonest and manipulative, but that is probably what made him so good at sales. And his tactics were probably an effective way to drive a sales team, but I sincerely believed that such tactics were the wrong way to run a software development team. Especially when doing something cutting-edge original, like we were doing, I think open and honest communications were extremely important. (I have worked with many companies where the sales team was both friendly and successful. One does not need to use abusive tactics to have success in sales. Indeed, the sales manager who relies on abuse is typically more interested in aggrandizing their own success, rather than the success of the company they work for.)

And my question was a valid one. He might have meant the previous September. Was he now saying that no one expected the team to be done this last September? Was he suddenly agreeing with me? Or did he mean to say "spring" and he accidentally said "September"? Both words start with "S" and I could imagine him mixing them up because he was angry. In my email, I had written "spring of 2016." This seemed like an important point to be clear on. If he was saying that he had never pressured us to be done during September, and I had imagined the pressure, then that would be a revelation.

"No one ever told you that! Whatever month you said, no one ever said that to you!"

If he meant "spring," then that was certainly true, but that is why I spoke up. Shouldn't estimates come from the tech team? There were really only two ways of interpreting our current situation:

One, Milburn was our real CEO and John was merely his assistant. If Milburn was our CEO, it was appropriate that he was generating our completion estimates and which tasks we needed to do. But in this scenario, we were a startup of just five people and yet we had gone almost six months without a single conversation between the CEO and the tech team.

Two, John was our CEO. Milburn was merely a member of the Board of Directors. In this scenario, we had daily conversations with our CEO, which was appropriate, but our board of directors, which should be merely advisory, was scheduling our deadlines, generating our estimates and even deciding which tasks we should put into PivotalTracker.

No matter which way we interpret this situation, something fundamentally irrational was happening.

I could imagine why Milburn might be in trouble with the other board members. Did he really think that because he wrote some Visual Basic code 15 years ago he was competent to estimate a cutting-edge NLP project in 2015? If so, this was perhaps an example of the Dunning-Kruger Effect, where someone with little knowledge of a subject doesn't realize how much they don't know and therefore assumes they are highly competent.

"I think the Spring of 2016 is a reasonable estimate for being feature complete and reliable," I offered.

"You will never say that again," Milburn snapped. "Do you hear me? You will never say that again. You have done everything in your power to demoralize this team. You have done everything in your power to distract them from the mission. You have done everything in your power to sabotage this project. I'm sick of it. I am sick of your bullshit. I am sick of your sabotage. You will never say that again, do you understand?"

I might have argued that is was his unrealistic deadlines that were demoralizing the team. Instead, I spread the blame over the whole board: "Fear is being communicated to the team by the board of directors."

Milburn did not take that well, either. "The board simply wants you to meet a deadline for once! You feel fear because we need you to live up to one of your deadlines?"

"We are on track to meet my estimated deadlines."

"Your estimates are bullshit! You keep telling John, 'I'll be done tomorrow,' and you never are!"

"Honest communication might clear up some of the confusion."

"EXCEPT *YOU* REFUSE TO BE HONEST WITH ANYONE!"

"Why were we not consulted about the change of direction in July? "

"THERE WAS NO CHANGE IN DIRECTION!"

"There was no change in direction back on July 28th?"

"DON'T TRY TO CHANGE THE SUBJECT! I AM SICK OF YOUR PSYCHOLOGICAL TRICKS!"

"My tricks?"

"YOU CRACKED UNDER THE PRESSURE OF A DEADLINE! THAT'S THE SUBJECT YOU WANT TO AVOID!"

"Why were we told some ridiculous story about Griffin and Dennis—"

"YOU CRACKED UNDER PRESSURE! YOU'RE NOT A MAN, YOU'RE A LITTLE BOY!"

"—and John? Why tell us that they went to a Salesforce convention and magically found—"

"YOU'RE A FRIGHTENED LITTLE BOY!"

"—some investors who were willing to write a check on the spot? Why not tell us the truth?"

"YOU'RE NOT FIT FOR LEADERSHIP! YOU'RE A FRIGHT-ENED LITTLE BOY!"

I wondered if his instincts told him to pre-emptively throw accusations at me before I could throw them at him.

A fascinating aspect of this whole conversation was that he never threatened to fire me. All of these threats and accusations were his way of motivating me to work harder. With almost scientific precision, he had moved through many of the same kinds of tactics that might have sucked a potential customer into committing to a purchase:

- First, he tried to get me to apologize for hurting his feelings, knowing that if I apologized for anything, then I would have to apologize for everything.
- He tried to shame me by insinuating that I was slowing down my coworkers. "You are wasting the time of your coworkers, when they are trying to stay focused on getting the next release out."
- Next he attacked my masculinity: "ARE YOU MAN ENOUGH TO ADMIT YOU FAILED?" Many men, especially younger men, might retort with something akin to, "Dammit, even if I have to work ninety hours a week, we are going to succeed!"
- That didn't work, so he switched tactics and tried to make me feel selfish and petty because I had offered an honest assessment of Sital: "You like to blame others, don't you?"
- None of that worked, so then he tried to get me to commit to something that he could use against me later, and when I didn't rise to the bait, he tried to pressure me into conceding that something was black and white, when it wasn't: "IT'S A YES OR NO QUESTION!"
- At that point I tried to raise the issue that John also needed to take some responsibility for the progress of the company, at

which point Milburn had tried to get me to take on a CTOs level of responsibility: "ONCE YOU RING THAT BELL YOU CAN'T UNRING IT!"

- Since I hadn't backed down, he switched tactics again, and focused on limiting what I was allowed to have any say over: "No one ever told you September."
- Finally he attacked my maturity, to imply that I had no authority to offer opinions about co-workers: "YOU'RE A FRIGHTENED LITTLE BOY!"

His tirade could be considered a master class in sales tactics, except those tactics were too obvious. The audience is not supposed to see how a magician performs his or her tricks. When I first read about him online, I assumed Milburn combined penetrating emotional insights with the expressive range of a great actor. But that was not what I had run into today. He really had just a handful of gambits, and he leaned on them too heavily, like a chef who tries to hide their mistakes by using a lot of salt.

By this point we had been talking for so long that it was time for the meeting with the entire team. We had to end our call.

I played a support role all day, helping Sital work through some of his errors, and then in the evening helping Gregory make some progress on the final confirmation stage of the Conversation FSM.

The project was enormous fun, but I didn't want to work with Milburn anymore, so at the end of the day, I called Mera. I let her know that things were going badly, and that I would need to find another job. I asked her to talk to John about the likelihood that I would be leaving.

FRIDAY, NOVEMBER 6TH, 2015

Over the next few days, we worked out the final bugs. We were able to send a message from the iPhone through the NLP model, back to the iPhone for confirmation, then to the server again, and then to Salesforce. This was similar to the demo we had on September 17, but now we had much more error protection, and the system was stable for a much wider set of possibilities. It was something we could actually put in a customer's hands. It was an exciting moment.

We had accomplished in three months what a truly elite team would have done in six weeks. We were struggling against some serious and truly bizarre personnel issues, however, so ours was a success story of which I was proud.

I spent the evening writing up long emails to Sital, Hwan, and Gregory, explaining to them everything I thought they would need to know. Then I wrote to Milburn and John confirming that it was my last day.

Sunday, November 8th, 2015

Look at a tree, then look away and try to sketch the tree from memory. Did you remember everything about the tree? Each leaf, each twig, the exact position of the bird's nest in the crown? There are innumerable small details.

Summing up months of difficult technical work is similar to sketching from memory. Inevitably, Gregory had dozens of questions about all the things I'd forgotten to write down. For the simple stuff he texted me, but some topics required more than a text. I realized I should work a few more days. Ideally, I could work as a freelance contractor, charging the hourly equivalent of what my salary had been. I sent John a text message, and later an email, suggesting this as a plan. I did not hear back from him.

Monday, November 9th, 2015

I realized I'd left some books at work, and I also wanted to talk to John about working on an hourly basis, so I headed back to the incubator. When I got there, I tried to use my security card to get in, but it didn't work. They'd certainly been fast about deactivating it.

I went over to the security desk to ask for a pass to go upstairs. There were two guards present: a gentleman who was sitting behind the desk, and a very large gentleman who was wearing a jacket that read security. Operating as if I had done this a hundred times, I calmly got out my ID and showed it to them.

The first gentleman looked up my name, then turned to the other guard and said, "It's him."

The larger man took his walkie-talkie and spoke into it. "You there?"

A voice on the other end said, "Yes?"

And the guard intoned into his walkie-talkie, "He's here."

I took a step back, furrowing my brow. What the hell?

The first guard jumped up from behind the desk and shouted at me, "You stand right there! Don't you dare move! Don't you dare!"

I wasn't sure what was going on, but I decided it would be best to leave and call a friend at the incubator to get the whole story. I could always come back later, better prepared—at the moment it seemed that something very weird was happening, and it was probably happening on terms that John and Milburn preferred.

"I'll just wait outside," I said.

"Don't you dare move!" shouted the guard again, but I knew they weren't police and thus had no authority to stop me. I headed for the door. A brief moment of paranoia hit me, and I wondered if I was being accused of something—so I listened carefully to whatever the security guards might say as I was leaving. But at no point did they say anything like, "Stop or we will call the police," or, "Stop, the police will be here soon!"

I left. They did not chase after me.

I walked to a cafe and called Varak. "Hi, Varak! It's Lawrence. How are you?"

He laughed. "Hey man, I'm good. Hang on a second. I can't talk right now. You Know Who is here."

"You Know Who?" I was confused. "John? You can't talk around John?"

Then he whispered, "No, it's the old guy."

"Ah!" I began to get the picture. "Milburn."

Varak was still whispering. "He's going to blow a gasket."

"Did something bad happen?"

"Didn't you quit?" he inquired pointedly.

"I sure did." Then I asked, "Is that what they're upset about?"

"They're a lot more than upset. Hang on a second, I'll take the phone closer to them."

I didn't hear anything for a minute. Then I heard a printer printing some documents, Vladimir asking a question, and Milburn in the back ground, far away but shouting, "You don't have a plan? You don't have a plan? You really screwed up this time, John, you really screwed up! You sabotaged us again!"

There were some banging sounds, and then Varak came back on the line, talking very softly. "I can't get any work done. The guy's been screaming for over an hour. I'm thinking of going to the NYU manager

137

who oversee the place and filing a complaint."

"Wow." I was so surprised by the gratuitous drama that I couldn't think of anything intelligent to say. "Wow."

"Have you had lunch?" he asked me in a low voice.

"No, are you free?"

"Meet me at that Vietnamese place in an hour."

I sent a text message to Gregory explaining the bad news to him. I probably wouldn't be allowed to work with him anymore.

Stress aside, the whole day was kind of hilarious. Folks from the incubator joined me for lunch at a Vietnamese pho place we favored. Vladimir attempted an imitation of Milburn, acting out his awkward rage, almost picking up a chair so he could … who knows. Express frustration? Varak did an imitation of John cowering in fear. Then an impression of Sital looking confused.

Eventually, I went home. I later sent a long email to Hwan explaining how insane the day had been. Hwan wrote back and told me that Milburn had issued all of them a warning that they could never talk to me again.

Though I felt loyal to Hwan and Gregory, they knew I would never get paid for helping them, so after that point they didn't send me any technical questions.

DECEMBER, 2015

I teamed up with a friend, and we started to explore the idea of building a voice interface for Salesforce. While doing the preliminary research, I realized that Amazon and Apple and IBM and Google were all racing to roll out voice recognition services. Clearly, it would be the next big thing, evolving rapidly, with firms announcing significant changes on nearly a monthly basis. The idea of a text interface has some upsides, but voice interfaces offer some real convenience. In particular, if a salesperson meets with Carol Harrington, who agrees to buy a million bottles of shampoo, then what the salesperson really wants to do is get in their car and drive home. If, while they drive, they can talk to their phone, and the phone puts all their data in Salesforce for them, then that is clearly a big win over both traditional graphical interfaces and text interfaces.

JANUARY, 2016

I went to Virginia to see some old friends, and on my way back I stopped through Washington, DC so Hwan and I could catch up. We met at a diner in the DC sprawl known as northern Virginia. He complained that the project was making slow progress and that John and Milburn were in an extremely negative mood. Gregory was still part time, and Hwan often found himself with nothing to do. If Hwan sent Gregory a request and Gregory had already hit the contractual limit for the number of hours he could work in a week, then Hwan would have to wait until the following week to get the change he needed.

At the same time, the sense of crisis was gone. Milburn now talked to the team twice a day, once in the morning and once in the evening. Apparently he was applying less pressure now that he felt fully informed about the team's progress. I was curious if he'd regained the faith of the board.

MARCH, 2016

I stopped through DC again, and Hwan and I caught up. He'd had his own bizarre confrontation with Milburn. Sital had been making constant mistakes, which broke the code, so Hwan again raised the issue of hiring someone better. Milburn got angry and accused Hwan of taking pleasure in blaming others. Milburn also said that most of the problems at Celolot could be traced back to Hwan's "terrible" iPhone app.

After that, Hwan started looking for his next job. He was interested in moving to Silicon Valley so that he could be at the heart of the tech industry.

What exactly was Sital doing? Hwan wasn't sure. What exactly was John doing? Hwan wasn't sure. We imagined those two sitting in the incubator, failing to make progress, as the days turned into weeks and the weeks turned into months. If we are what we do, as the expression goes, then Sital had become one of the world's very few professional YouTube watchers. Perhaps he had now watched every playthrough of every Zelda game and every possible weightlifting video. Perhaps one day he will have watched every single video on YouTube. On that day, with nothing more to watch, perhaps he will finally get to work.

APRIL, 2016

The second Big Pivot. To his credit, Milburn came up with an idea that was truly audacious. He no longer wanted to just work on integration with SalesForce. Instead, he envisioned a general framework that would allow the NLP engine to be applied to any schema in any database. If he could pull it off, he would accomplish a very important breakthrough.

The project was now very much in the territory of a pure research project. I'd love to lead such a project, but I would demand a team of five excellent programmers, and I would need a full year. And there would be no guarantee of success.

As Hwan told me about this, I first thought "What an idiot! Didn't Milburn learn anything from the fiasco of the first Big Pivot?" But later I realized that Milburn knew what he was doing. All through the summer, autumn, and winter they'd been thinking they were about to get more money from investors. Apparently every deal had fallen through. At this point they'd been fundraising for nearly two years, using the idea of "NLP for Salesforce." Investors had grown wary, perhaps because Celolot had made no progress, or perhaps because Tactile.com was doing so much better.

This new idea was audacious in ways that might bring in a new crop of suckers. And sure enough, Milburn would eventually close a deal.

Or it's possible Milburn simply got lucky. I am perhaps giving him too much credit. A different interpretation of events suggests that he simply gets bored of projects, just like my ex–business partner in Virginia. Lacking discipline, he might be the type who is good at coming up with ideas, but terrible at turning them into reality.

June, 2016

I stopped through DC again, so Hwan and I met for lunch. He had just gotten a job with a startup in Silicon Valley, and he would be moving out there by July. Milburn had been surprisingly calm when Hwan announced that he was leaving.

Celolot had hired two remote programmers who reported to Sital. For all practical purposes, Sital had become the CTO. I thought this was surely the most bizarre bit of news I was going to hear during the year of 2016, but eventually the American presidential election beat it.

As far as I know, Celolot continues to make progress at a glacial pace. Despite having an app that only works with iPhones, they no longer have an iPhone developer on staff. Maybe they eventually gave up on the iPhone app.

September, 2016

Varak was working at the incubator. John came in elated and told him "We just raised $2.5 million dollars! We were down to our last $1,000, and we closed a deal for $2.5 million!"

Varak told me about this conversation later.

Is it true they were down to their last $1,000? Is it true they received $2.5 million? With Celolot, it was always a bit tricky to tell what was real and what was a smokescreen. I believe they did raise more funds, but as to whether they were down to their last $1,000, that sounds exactly like the kind of needlessly dramatic detail that Milburn would invent and then tell to an always gullible John.

October, 2016

Varak had fallen in love with a girl in Sweden, so he was moving there. Meanwhile, Lee's girlfriend was waiting patiently in his native Canada. They'd decided their time in New York was over, and they held a going-away party at the photography studio in Brooklyn that Lee had rented for the previous ten years.

I went and saw several familiar faces. At some point I offered praise for the ability of the NYU incubator to bring people together. In response, Varak snorted, and said it was a terrible incubator because it lacked a sense of community.

"But here we are," I said.

"What do you mean?" he asked.

"Look around the room. I've worked at very few places where I'd want to invite all of my co-workers to a personal party. But here we are."

He conceded that that was true but insisted that TechStars, where he'd been previously, was still a much better incubator.

Leandor of G-Code, the startup focused on teaching girls how to code, was there. She'd been to Y Combinator, and she said that the NYU incubator couldn't hold a candle to her experience in Silicon Valley. Although she disagreed with some of the things the leadership of Y Combinator said, the community itself was amazing. The alumni who emerged from the experience stuck together and really supported each other.

Okay, so let us suppose that all of that was true. Let's believe for a moment that the NYU incubator was the worst incubator in the world. To me, that seems like a very powerful argument in favor of such places. As I've said before, much of my previous experience building software startups had involved grinding isolation and loneliness. Being at the NYU incubator was an absolute treat. If it offered a below-average experience, then surely all software startups should be in an incubator, because even the bad incubators are much better than any alternative.

December, 2016

Tactile.com announced that they had raised an additional $15 million and were going to build a voice interface for Salesforce. It was exactly what my friend and I had looked into doing the previous December, but we had lacked the money to pull it off.

January, 2017

Apparently they never got that $2.5 million dollars. Once again, they had been over-confident about their ability to close a round of funding. Out of money, the company was on life-support. The Board Of Directors put in another $200,000 to keep things going for a little while longer.

From this point forward the smart play was to find that unusual customer who needed the app exactly the way it was now, with no additional features. If only they could close two or three big sales, then Celolot would seem viable, at which point the company itself could be sold, and the investors could recoup some of their losses, or even make a small profit.

But they were not able to close any sales. For a company run by a fellow who used to be a top salesman, there was a strange failure to hit any goals.

March, 2017

Around this time, Sital disappeared from the office. Presumably the Board Of Directors was tired of paying an incompetent. Blame should be split evenly between Sital and the Board Of Directors. The original strategy had been to hire an inexperienced programmer who was cheap, but also

143

an expensive consultant who was experienced (Arthur). There is nothing wrong with that strategy. It could have worked if Sital had been ambitious and hungry to learn. Instead, he wasted the opportunity. That was his fault. But then, the Board should have been ready to fire him in the autumn of 2015. Waiting an additional 18 months is unforgivable.

JUNE, 2017

Time erases lies. When I first joined Celolot in the spring of 2015, I assumed that John was being paid at least as well as I was, because he was the CEO. Now I know he was never the real CEO. In Washington D.C., in the summer of 2014, he'd worked as an intern for Milburn. I'm sure he was then paid starvation wages, though possibly he was given a bonus for each sale he made -- that is a common deal for salespeople.

Likely he was hired as a salesperson for Celolot. I now suspect he was offered a pathetic base salary, plus a percentage of sales. That would explain his desperation for sales in 2015. A little bit of poverty can make a person ambitious, but too much poverty simply causes people to become angry, and then apathetic.

Both Milburn and John had deluded themselves with the idea that the project would be easy and sales would be immediate and large. In their minds, they were already spending the vast treasure they assumed they would have by the late summer of 2015. Like stepping into a shower and confusing the hot water handle for the cold, the gush of reality was a startling shock.

I've seen these kinds of wild daydreams undermine many otherwise promising startups. I would urge all entrepreneurs to be cautious. Even when a business does well, it's often two or three years before there is serious money coming in.

And who can spend their life pushing against stone? Utterly exhausted, John attempted to quit, but the Board Of Directors invoked some obscure part of his contract, which frightened him into working for awhile longer.

But the thing about reality is that it always wins in the end.

SEPTEMBER, 2017

Out of money, Celolot disappeared from the incubator.

I am both saddened and frustrated. I continue to believe in the basic idea that animated Celolot. For me, the project was tremendous fun. I love the excitement of a difficult technological problem which might help solve a real problem.

The problem remains. Most sales software is disliked by staff that is forced to use it. Most sales managers spend their time harassing employees to document their encounters with potential leads. An NLP interface would make it easier for people to record their activities. Increased participation would improve the efficiency of teams. It is a billion dollar idea and some day someone will do it right. And they will become immensely rich.

To his credit, Milburn was a bit ahead of the curve when he came up with the idea for Celolot back in 2014. But when it comes to startups, what matters is execution, not ideas. And his execution was terrible. His transactional mindset is sometimes successful in sales roles, but it does not translate to leadership roles. Leaders needs to think long-term. They need to build healthy relationships that can survive the crisis of the moment. Creating a business is always a marathon, it is never a sprint. Outside of sales, the transactional mindset tends to be a liability.

NOVEMBER, 2017

I wrote to Steve, the guy who was in charge of the incubator. I let him know about the arrival of the first edition of this book.

APRIL, 2018

Steve and I caught up for lunch. Vignettes from the life of the incubator were tallied for their humor, but also their contribution to the economy. How many jobs have been created? How much revenue? NYU had just released its study regarding the impact of the incubator: "3,200 jobs and $4 billion for New York."

Some wonderful characters have passed through the incubator. A few stories were hilarious. Perhaps one or two will have historic importance. We agreed that startups can be stressful and so it is natural that strong personalities will clash. It's all part of the life of startups.

EPILOGUE

Humans are messy. They have emotions, and emotions are messy. Startups are made of humans. Therefore startups are messy. (It's the Transitive Property Of Startups.)

Every startup has a unique mix of strengths and weaknesses. Celolot is lucky enough to be lead by a goal-oriented salesperson—sometimes that is a great advantage. Will it be an advantage in an industry that is mostly about developing a specific technological breakthrough? Time will tell.

Many times, when people launch a new startup, they worry, "But what if Google or Amazon decides to compete with us? They will crush us!" This fear rarely has any merit. When a startup dies, the vast majority of the time the cause is suicide, not homicide. If one can avoid self-sabotage then one's chances of success are dramatically increased.

The tech industry uses the phrase "Anti-Pattern" to refer to worst practices that are best avoided. I saw several Anti-Patterns at Celolot that I've also seen at other startups, including my own. Drawing from this cumulative experience, the following three are the Anti-Patterns I highly recommend if you are hoping for failure:

1.) Don't ever fire anyone.

Companies need to be aggressive about firing weak players. I have never seen a company that was aggressive enough. Managers always wait too long, for one of several reasons:

- *Compassion*: this is rare, but sometimes managers worry about a worker, or their family, and hesitate to fire them out of concern.
- *Ego*: more common. If the manager or their lieutenant hired a weak player, they won't want to admit they made a mistake. They might even give the weak player a promotion, to hide the fact that they made a mistake.
- *Cowardice*: even more common. Firing people involves a lot of messy emotions, including anger and hate and fear, plus it sparks a craving for revenge, so most managers avoid it as long as possible.

I will never know why Celolot hung on to Sital. Possibly our "brilliantly creative data scientist of incredible genius" was a pawn in a game Milburn was running on unwary investors. Or perhaps John was simply a coward and didn't like direct confrontation. It's also possible that Milburn's ego was such that he refused to admit they'd made a mistake—the more I criticized Sital, the more determined Milburn was to hang on to him. And of course, there might have been some reality to the defense they offered: that they thought they were about to get more money, and so they really did think they could dump Sital soon. Or perhaps they never truly understood how much Sital had slowed the project down. There is some evidence for each of these theories. It's possible that all them are a little bit true.

(This rule doesn't apply to large, stable companies, as workers have a right to enjoy their lives outside of work. In fact, stable companies might well have apprenticeship programs that can and should accommodate beginners such as Sital. But if we are talking about a startup that has zero revenue, an unwillingness to fire weak players is an excellent way to doom the ship.)

2.) Lie to everyone about everything.

Circumstances usually force entrepreneurs to lie. Perhaps we should use the polite term "exaggerate." Those of us starting a business exaggerate our chances of success so that investors will give us money. We exaggerate our current success so that suppliers will trust us with credit. We exaggerate our certainty so that workers will feel safe committing their time to us. We are constantly selling, not just to customers, but to every group that we interact with. Building confidence is a hustle.

However, the correct ratio is typically something like ninety-nine percent truth and one percent lie. The more we tell the truth the more people trust us and thus the more power we have when we need to lie. Lying indiscriminately, all the time, to everyone, simply alienates people. Lies need to be reserved for the decisive moments.

On cutting edge technical projects, it is absolutely essential to have honest communication between the tech team and the leadership. Otherwise, one is sailing a ship over rough corals, without charts and without a compass. Only a miracle will get you to the other side.

3.) Insist that the project is easy.

If you really want to destroy your startup, you should assume that you know everything about the problem you're facing. Assume that you know what your customers want and how they will react to your product. Assume that building the product is straightforward. And most importantly, any time you encounter a problem, remember that you can make it go away by telling your workers that it is easy.

One of the most powerful habits of self-sabotage is the idea that a leader can leave a novel project to their assistant. This works fine so long as assistant is very smart, very ambitious and is granted complete autonomy. But often those in leadership positions want to hang on to the power to veto decisions. It's this veto that does all the damage. Many times, after hundreds of hours of careful study, the assistant will realize that a strategy that sounds counter-intuitive is in fact the best course of action. The leader will then veto the idea because the strategy does not sound promising after a superficial glance. Only by investing hundreds of hours of study does one realize why the "wrong" strategy is actually the right one. So long as the leader thinks the project is "easy," they don't see why they should invest hundreds of hours of study.

Any economic boom that lasts long enough eventually draws in amateurs who have a bit of money to invest. Most of them suffer from the Dunning-Kruger Effect—they don't know enough to understand how little they know. Milburn failed to understand how much he failed to understand about NLP. His ignorance lead him to assume not only that the project would be easy, but also that he knew everything he needed to know. That is almost always a fatal assumption. Even though I have close to two decades of experience in the industry, I'm palpably aware of how important it is to approach each new startup with the assumption that I don't know half the things I need to know.

How to strengthen the startup culture in the United States

If you read much of the business press, you're aware that there are two competing theories about what makes a great business leader. One theory says that leaders should be extremely aggressive psychopaths who crush all their competition. For an example of this theory, you can read almost any biography about Steve Jobs. The second theory says that humble, egoless leaders build the most successful companies, because they do the best job facilitating cooperation and communication. James Collins, in his book *Good to Great*, makes this case about several leaders, including Darwin E. Smith of the paper company Kimberly-Clark.

We can find examples of both types of leaders succeeding. Steve Jobs was successful. So was Darwin E. Smith. Is there any way to reconcile the conflicting theories? I believe there is: simply assume that the most important quality that any business leader can have is the willingness to quickly fire weak players. Therefore, ruthless psychopaths damage their businesses with their pathology, but make up for it by firing people quickly. Humble, egoless leaders help their companies with their healthy attitudes, but undermine the business by being too slow to fire weak players.

Humble, egoless leadership, ready to fire fast—that is a rare combination. I would say that Andy Grove of Intel had that combination of traits. And of course, there is Ray Kroc of McDonald's. Due to some people's aversion to the food sold at McDonald's, the sheer brilliance of Kroc's entrepreneurship often goes unsung. But he was willing to take a risk on complete unknowns, most notably on June Martino, one of the all-time greatest hires in the history of American business. (Her hire also led to an important moment in feminism: Martino was granted a reasonable block of equity in McDonald's before their IPO, thus becoming the first woman in history to be treated as a true co-founder of a startup.) At the same time, Kroc was willing to fire anyone who didn't work out. That combination of willingness to take risks on unknowns and quickly fire any mistakes is something to which all business leaders should aspire.

How to spread awareness of what leading a startup requires?

Recently, I exchanged some email with my friend Colin Steele, currently CTO of TypeZero and formerly CTO of RoomKey.com. We discussed another startup that had failed, and he wrote:

> It's sad and disheartening. I think few people understand how amazingly difficult it is to start a new business, and run it successfully. Drama, people, and personalities, seem to have an outsized role in how these things crash and burn. There needs to be some codification of best internal practices for creating startups, like Steve Blank's book "4 Steps To The Epiphany," but for the culture; a co-routine that runs alongside "customer development"—call it "culture development" or something.

I agree wholeheartedly, and would also add that more public discussion of the difficulties would help startup culture. I would make an analogy to the history of divorce in the United States. The divorce rate rose for much of the twentieth century, and it peaked in the 1970s and 1980s. Since then there has been more public discussion about what makes marriages strong. You can see the trend reflection on television shows: neither Leave It To Beaver nor the Brady Bunch mentioned the difficulties of marriage, and that was the era when the divorce rate was rising the most. Modern sitcoms talk endlessly about the difficulties of marriage. Couples still face drama and conflict and personality, but the public discussion seems to have granted people the vocabulary they need to address their problems, and the divorce rate has come down. Popular awareness helps. At the very least, books and movies can help explore the important reality that startups are not easy.

Is the struggle worth it? We never get all of the facts, but history teaches us that it is safer to create the future than to defend the past. More so, we will never fully understand the motivations of other people, but we do not need to. It is enough to understand ourselves. Our own relationship to action tells us who we are, and the results of our efforts reveal to us our creative potential. A startup is an adventure that beckons: you sign up, you set sail, you do battle, circumstance forces a decision, and in the end the only part of the story you can be entirely sure of is the part that you saw with your own eyes.

Responses To Others

Some readers have sent me email, others have posted reviews at places like Amazon and Goodreads. I want to respond to two.

By some wild coincidence, John Leimgruber stumbled upon my book. He had been hired at the startup in Virginia which I mention in my introduction. He was hired sometime after I left in 2008. A few years later he quit and moved north. He wrote to me after he'd read my book. I host a once-a-month dinner party at my place in Manhattan, so I invited him over and we were able to meet and compare notes about some of the absurdity we'd seen in the startup world. Many people asked a particular question of me, but Leimgruber phrased it best, in his review on Amazon, so I quote him here, to answer everyone:

> Personally, I find the book most interesting not for the absurdly lousy management characters, but for giving a glimpse into the mind of a person that accepts this kind of treatment as okay, shoulders unreasonable burdens, and seems repeatedly drawn into difficult situations with the corresponding drama that inevetibly ensues.
>
> This begs the question for me (and likely much of this book's readership):
>
> Why are many talented software developers drawn to solving impossible problems, drinking unhealthy amounts of coffee, neglecting their sleep and personal lives, and constantly trying to fix everthing and everyone around them while ignoring their own psychosocial needs?

To my mind, the interesting question runs in the other direction. Why i bad leadership so common? Why is it so universally accepted? To anyon who suggests that we should quit our jobs after some disagreements wit management, I would ask why is it that we need to leave? Why doesn't th leadership leave? Shouldn't management resign, if they are unfit to get th mission done?

Some questions have large implications. Why are so many leaders s completely self-destructive? If Milton had simply been greedy, in a rational way, he would have allowed me to work on the technology that might have eventually generated a lot of money for him. But I find that business leaders are rarely rational. Impulses and ego seem to be the most common forms of decision making. Why is this accepted?

My story was discussed on Hacker News, and the most common advice given was "Lawrence should have quit much sooner." Is that true? I was only there for six months. It was a job that paid reasonably, in the low six figures, and I was working on some cutting edge issues that the tech industry was just beginning to take seriously, and I was at a startup incubator full of amazing people. This last point was perhaps hidden during editing. Those people thrilled me. In the rough draft to this manuscript I included a lot of detail about the other people in the incubator, however, myself and my editors cut most of that material so that this book would remain short and focused. But the other people at that incubator were certainly among the attractions. I've remained good friends with a few of them.

The second comment I'd like to respond to was written by "Antoni" on Goodreads:

> I loved the first 80% of it, which is enough to give a positive opinion I guess. What I didn't like really is that the book is written from the perspective of startup employee, not the founder. So there's only part of the story. Only information that the writer assumes. He uses a lot of exaggerations as well that are fun to read and enjoyable but some dialogues are hard to believe to be true.

> I would recommend it to people working in tech startups, to feel good about the environment that they work for rather than take some valuable lesson from the book since it's more about management tyranny, mobbing and lack of transparency rather than actual reasons why startup failed from a perspective of a person that had full picture (instead of an employee).

In response, please consider these four ideas:

1.) The failure of any venture is always a complex event, and no one can easily say why it failed. Consider when an airplane crashes, it often takes an army of investigators years to figure out why the accident occurred, even though the investigators are guided by the experience of all previous airplane failures. A startup with an entirely novel idea will be too unique for anyone to easily diagnose its failure. There are too many variables, and too many embedded assumptions.

2.) A good leader over-communicates in a crisis, and every day is a new crisis for a startup. Above all else, the leadership needs to "listen real loud." A startup is either a transparent learning organization or it is dead. Milton's crass hoarding of secrets was a self-inflicted injury. While there might be some other reasons why the startup failed, it is absolutely true that our lack of communication was the starting point of all the other problems that we faced. Since I was central to the technology effort, the startup could only succeed if I was well-informed about our real needs. Keeping me in the dark was a problem for the whole company. I'm confused how anyone could complain that this book is about "lack of transparency rather than the actual reasons why the startup failed." I've tried to be clear about this, but I'll repeat it here again: lack of transparency was one of the reasons why the startup failed. We can debate whether it was the most important factor, but it was obviously a significant factor.

3.) Antoni says they wished the book was told "from the perspective of a person that had the full picture (instead of an employee)." Possibly I failed to emphasize this enough, but no one at Celelot had the full picture. Just like the three blind men in the fable, we were each touching a different part of the elephant, and we were reaching different conclusions about its shape. I was holding onto the technology, so I believed one thing, while Milton was holding onto the sales leads, so he believed something else. This much is completely normal at all businesses, it is a problem with a standard solution: lots of honest communication. Sadly, honesty was lacking. A series of lies were told about the company's finances, so myself and Kwan were constantly guessing at the truth. At some points we felt we were working at a well-capitalized firm, other times we thought the whole place was about to run out of money. But neither Milton nor John knew much about the company, either. At no point did Milton sit down and have a good faith conversation with me about the status of the code at the company. At first I was elated with the level of autonomy I'd been granted, then later I realized that the leadership was operating with assumptions that were out of line with reality. A ship captain who has no idea of their location near the coast is a ship captain who is about to run aground, and likewise, Milton's ignorance of our progress meant the whole company was slipping toward hidden reefs. If Milton were to write a book about Celelot, he could fill in his side of things, but his side of things would not represent the total truth.

4.) We have suffered a glut of books that aim to build a cult of personality around certain entrepreneurs. This tendency has gone furthest with Steve

Jobs. What is remarkable is that this trend should get going at a time when innovation from Silicon Valley is clearly decreasing. In his 2006 book, The HP Way, David Packard talks about the process by which he and Bill Hewlett grew Hewlett–Packard. In their rejection of standard corporate hierarchies and their hunger for input from everyone, they were clearly blazing a radically new path in both management style and technology. It is noteworthy that when they were at their most creative, in the 1940s and 1950s and 1960s, no one set out to create a cult of personality around them. In 1968, when Robert Noyce and Gordon Moore founded Intel, no one thought to write them up as heroic characters, but it was in that era that their technology was creating the most profound shifts in industry. At some point after 2000 the rate of innovation in Silicon Valley began to slow, and yet this was the era when the rhetoric about visionary geniuses and innovation began to take on the tone formerly reserved for artists and military conquerors. Real leadership is rare, so we should celebrate it whenever it appears, but we should remember it comes as often from the lower ranks as the upper ranks, so a series of books that only looks at the upper ranks must automatically leave us with a skewed picture of reality. My point is, we need more honesty about what is actually happening in these companies. We need less books written by or about founders, and more books written by those who are in the trenches, working everyday to build something new. Above all else, we need better documentation of the ways that management often sabotages the worker's efforts to invent the future.

ENDNOTES

1. Baer, Drake. "Why Data God Jeffrey Hammerbacher Left Facebook To Found Cloudera." Fast Company. May 03, 2013. Accessed July 28, 2017. https://www.fastcompany.com/3008436/takeaway/why-data-god-jeffrey-hammerbacher-left-facebook-found-cloudera

2. Bhatti, Jay. "Is The Varick Street NYU Poly Incubator The Best In NYC?" http://www.businessinsider.com/is-the-varick-street-nyu-poly-incubator-the-best-in-nyc-2011-10

3. Jarmul, Katharine. "Embedded *isms in Vector-Based Natural Language Processing." Kjamistan. September 16, 2016. Accessed July 27, 2017. http://kjamistan.com/embedded-isms-in-vector-based-natural-language-processing/

4. Koetsier, John. "CRM Sucks, but Voice, Messaging, AI, and $15 Million Could Make it Better." VentureBeat. December 13, 2016. Accessed July 27, 2017. https://venturebeat.com/2016/12/13/crm-sucks-but-voice-messaging- ai-and-15-million-could-make-it-better/

5. Drucker, Peter. *Innovation and Entrepreneurship*. HarperCollins US, 2011.

6. Krubner, Lawrence. "Object Oriented Programming is an Expensive Disaster Which Must End." Smash Company. October 7, 2014 Accessed July 27, 2017. http://www.smashcompany.com/technology/object-oriented-programming-is-an-expensive-disaster-which-must end

7. Drucker, *Innovation and Entrepreneurship*, 69.

ACKNOWLEDGEMENTS

Leah McCloskey is a graphic designer of great skill and patience. She helped us work through a dozen different ideas for a book cover. We are very pleased with her final creation.

Emi Lotto helped us with the actual technical details of putting the book in a format ready to be published. We are very grateful for her help.

Blanche Krubner, who has worked as an editor on over a dozen books, brought her skills to bear to be sure the sentences in this book make sense. We are very grateful for her help.

We would also like to thank our uniquely talented editor. We are endlessly in her debt for the wealth of insights she offered us regarding structure, voice and dialogue. She clarified for us when we should expand an obscure anecdote and when we should cut something too verbose. The book is vastly better thanks to her.